Following JESUS

The Life of a Disciple

Dr. Jeffrey T. Benda

Following Jesus: The Life of a Disciple

ISBN 978-0-9989982-0-6

Editing by ChristianEditingServices.com.

TABLE OF CONTENTS

FOREWORD

Years ago, I had the good fortune of hiring Jeff Benda to our church staff. It was one of the best hires I ever made. It wasn't just that Jeff was hard working and capable. He was certainly that. But what made Jeff effective for the small group ministry he helped to lead and for many individuals in our church was his passion for discipleship. You see, Jeff was not interested in merely running a church program. He was focused on intentionally discipling men and women and launching them out with deep spiritual conviction and influence as devoted Jesus followers.

Year after year Jeff did not waver in this "life on life" investment. It stayed as his first priority above all the other work he was asked to do at the church. And it paid off with big results. It changed lives with a lasting impact. I still run into men Jeff discipled while he was here in Little Rock. They all are marked by him with a deep rootedness in the Bible, but most of all, by a deep love for Jesus and a pursuit to be the man He wants them to be. These spiritual transformations all started with Jeff's investment in helping these men be disciples of the Lord Jeff loves.

I tell you all this so that you can know this book study, **Following Jesus**, is not some academic exercise. It is not wishful theory. It is, in fact, the personal notes of a disciplemaking veteran, drawn from the Bible, and crafted out of thousands of hours of real life, disciple-making interaction. In other words, this is a proven, disciple-making handbook. I've personally seen its fruit!

That's why I can highly recommend this study to you. I know the man. He's the real deal. Jesus said, "Go and make disciples." Jeff has! And with **Following Jesus** in your hands, so can you.

Dr. Robert Lewis
Little Rock, Arkansas

PREFACE

Jesus is the most unique person ever to live. He is both fully God and fully man. God the Father sent him to earth for a purpose: to pay the penalty for our sins so that we could establish a relationship with God.

When someone embraces Jesus Christ as Savior and God, that person becomes a disciple of Jesus. What are the expectations for a disciple of Jesus? What marks a person as a disciple of Jesus? How can a person grow to be like Jesus in all areas of life?

This eleven-week study is intended to be an introduction to what it means to be a disciple of Jesus. It will explain discipleship and provide the basic skills required to follow Jesus well. Once you have gone through this material, you can lead someone else through it, so that our faith can spread to others and we can help make disciples of Jesus together.

Following Jesus with you,

Jeff

WEEK
1

WHY DID JESUS COME?

Introduction: As we begin our journey of discipleship to Jesus, we must start by answering the question, "Why did Jesus come to earth?" As we seek to understand what the Bible says about this topic, we will also see that Jesus was not an ordinary man. He is God the Son, and his successful ministry changes everything!

1. **Look up John 1:1. What three statements are made about Jesus? What do you think those statements mean?**

   A. ______________________________

   B. ______________________________

   C.. ______________________________

WEEK 1 - MEMORY VERSES
John 10:10, 17:3

2. **Why might Jesus be referred to as the "Word"? (See Hebrews 1:1–3)**

____

____

Author and scholar R. C. H. Lenski writes, "Here already we may define the Logos-title: the Logos ('Word') is the final and absolute revelation of God, embodied in God's own Son, Jesus Christ. Christ is the Logos because in him all the purposes, plans, and promises of God are brought to a final focus and an absolute realization."[1]

THE WORD

In the beginning was the Word, and the Word was with God, and the Word was fully God.

— John 1:1

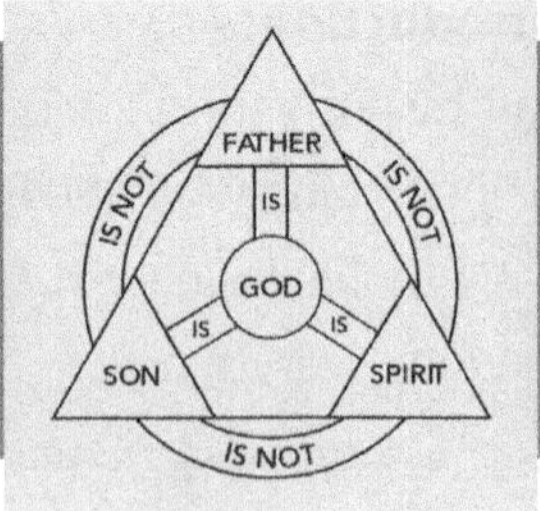

3. **How do the following notes on this verse help clarify John's meaning of Jesus as the "Word"?**

"A word serves two distinct purposes: a.) it gives expression to the inner thought, . . . and b.) it reveals this thought . . . to others. Christ is the Word of God in both respects."[2]

"Jesus, the Word (John 1:14), was not only God, but he was the expression of God to humankind. Jesus' life and ministry expressed to humankind what God wanted us to know."[3]

____

____

____

4. **Look up John 1:14 and Hebrews 2:14–17. What do we learn about the "Word" in these passages?**

In addition to being God the Son and the expression of God the Father by his words and actions, Jesus is also man. He is full deity and full humanity. As God the Son, Jesus took on flesh for a purpose.

5. **What does John 10:10 say about the purpose of Jesus' coming?**

6. **What do you think Jesus means by *life* in John 10:10?**

There are three primary Greek words translated ***life*** in the New Testament. Although the meanings of the words overlap, there does seem to be a specific emphasis for each word:

> ***Bíos*** from which we get our English word ***biology***. It refers to physical existence.[4]
>
> ***Psuché*** which refers to the immaterial part of humans, our soul.[5]
>
> ***Zōē*** a different word used by Jesus in John 10:10 to specifically express a new dimension to life that only he can bring. We will discover its meaning in a moment.

7. **John uses the word *zōē* (life) thirty-seven times in his Gospel. In seventeen of those usages, he includes the word *eternal*. Look up the following verses to understand what Jesus means by the use of *zōē*:**

    A. John 1:4 ____

    B. John 3:15–16 ____________________________________

    C. John 5:24 ____

8. **What do you think Jesus means in John 17:1–3 by the description of eternal life?**

    ____

    ____

    ____

This description of life is another use of the word ***zōē***. It is describing relational life with God. Eternal life refers not just to life that lasts forever but a relationship with God that lasts forever![6]

9. **In summary, John uses zōē to describe life as God designed it:**
   - the kind of life that God the Father and God the Son possess
   - life that is eternal in nature
   - life in addition to the physical and soul life a person possesses at birth
   - something God wants to give us freely!
   - a fullness of life that comes only from being relationally connected to God!

10. **If we are born with *bíos* (body) and *psuché* (soul), why are we not born with *zōē* (life)? How does Genesis 2:15–17 answer that question?**

____

____

____

11. **What do you think the Bible means by death?**

____

____

____

DEATH

In the Bible, death has temporal and eternal consequences. Temporally, it refers to the fear, guilt, blame, aimlessness, frustration, and enslaving habits we experience now because we live independently of God. Eternally, it describes a permanent separation from God in a place called hell.

According to *The Essential Bible Companion*, "Adam and Eve were put in Eden to be with God and in relationship with Him. Unfortunately, the path of disobedience led to the rupture of the relationship and the loss of access to God's presence."[7]

12. If Jesus came to give us *zōē* life, how does that help us with the problem of a lost relational connection to God as a result of the fall in the Garden of Eden (John 17:3)?

ZŌĒ LIFE

It [zōē life] is not just unending life. . . . Rather it is a quality of life . . . derived from a relationship with God. Having eternal life is here defined as being in relationship with the Father, the one true God, and Jesus Christ whom the Father sent.[8]

13. What has impacted you about the concept of *zōē* life?

14. How can you receive the gift of *zōē* life according to John 20:30–31?

- Come to Jesus alone for eternal life.
- Choose to embrace him as Savior and God by admitting you are sinful and need his forgiveness.
- As part of your choice to receive his gift of forgiveness and life, you must also choose to follow him as his disciple because he is God.

15. Have you embraced Jesus as Savior? Are you also following him and seeking to live life his way since he is God? Explain.

WEEK
2

The Primary Purpose of the Church

Introduction: Confusion abounds regarding the real purpose of the church. Understanding what, exactly, the church is will help to clarify its purpose. This lesson will seek to identify some of the descriptions of the church and Christ's expectations for it. These observations will help us determine what the church should be focused on as its primary ministry.

1. **In your opinion, what is the primary purpose of the church?**

____

____

2. **What common understandings do people have today related to the purpose of the church?**

____

____

WEEK 2 - MEMORY VERSES
Matthew 28:19–20

CHURCH AS THE BODY

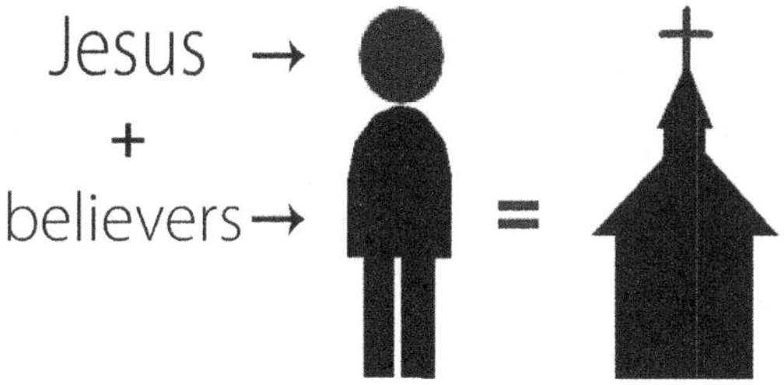

Diagram 1

3. How do the following verses describe the church?

Ephesians 1:22–23 (see Diagram 1)

____

Ephesians 2:19–22 (see Diagram 2)

____

Ephesians 3:1–6

____

CHURCH AS A TEMPLE

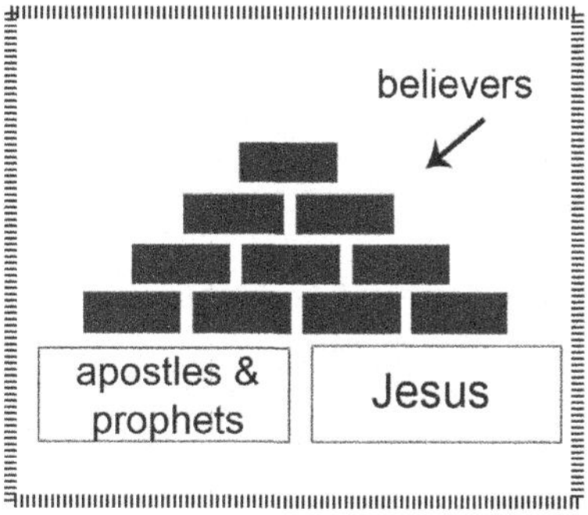

Diagram 2

4. **From what you learned in the verses above, how would you define success for the church?**

Christians are described as the body of Christ with Christ as the head. That means we are to live under his authority and leadership. We are also described as a temple, indicating that the Holy Spirit resides within us and we are to be holy as he is holy. We also see here that the church is built upon the foundation of Jesus as the Cornerstone as well as upon the teaching of the apostles and prophets. Finally, Christians are to be unified in their love for one another.

5. **Why did Jesus leave us here and not take us home when we embraced him as our Savior and God?**

6. **Read Matthew 28:18–20. How does this passage relate to the purpose of the church?**

7. **What is the command in the Great Commission?**

In his commentary on Matthew, Dr. Michael J. Wilkins writes, "The Great Commission contains one primary central command, the imperative 'make disciples,' with three subordinate participles, 'go,' 'baptizing,' and 'teaching.' The imperative explains the central thrust of the commission while the participles describe the process."[1]

8. In light of the clarification of the grammar of the passage, summarize the author's intent in your own words.

____

____

____

9. Who should make disciples? Explain.

____

____

10. Read Acts 11:26, 2 Corinthians 1:8, and John 1:12. How do those verses help us understand who should make disciples?

____

____

____

In Acts 11:26, the disciples are first called Christians. This is important because the word ***disciple*** is not used after the book of Acts. The word ***disciple*** is transitioned to other words in the New Testament. Some of those words are ***Christian***, ***believer***, ***brother***, and ***sister***. Since the word *disciple* is equivalent to *Christian*, all Christians need to be making disciples.

11. **Read Acts 1:8. What can we learn about the purpose of the church from this verse?**

    ____

    ____

12. **How does the following quote relate to the purpose of the church?**

    ____

    ____

In *Following the Master: A Biblical Theology of Discipleship*, Dr. Wilkins writes, "Discipleship is not just a limited program within the church. Discipleship is the life of the church. Since the true church is composed only of disciples, the overall activities of the church are to provide for the care, training, and mission of the disciples as they follow Jesus in this world. The purpose and mission of the church, therefore, must be understood in terms of **comprehensive discipleship.**"[2]

13. **In the above quote, what do you think the author means by "comprehensive discipleship"?**

    ____

    ____

    ____

COMPREHENSIVE DISCIPLESHIP

"I am aware that discipleship in the way that Jesus directed it is much more multidimensional. Jesus impacted the whole person in every area of life. When I am helping someone to grow as a disciple, I must also help that person develop in every area of life."[3]

— Wilkins

14. What core discipleship values should we have as a church family to encourage comprehensive discipleship to Jesus?

____

____

____

____

15. Read the following verses and use one word to summarize each reference with a core value.

Hebrews 12:28 ______________________

1 Peter 2:17 ______________________

2 Peter 3:18 ______________________

Ephesians 4:11–12 ______________________

INTEGRATED DISCIPLESHIP

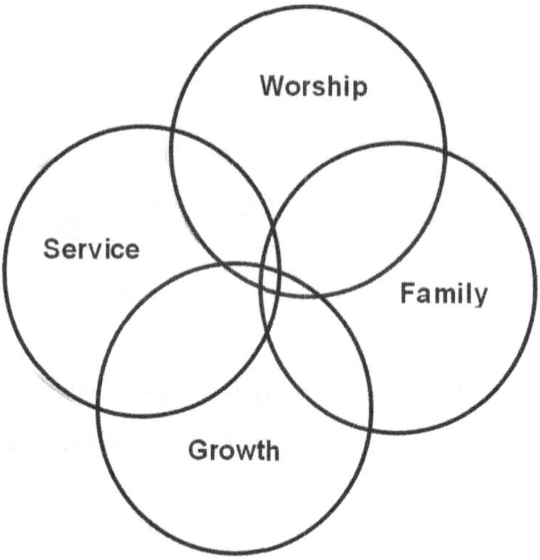

16. In relation to what we have discussed in this lesson, what do you think Jesus expects of you and me as disciples?

____

____

Comprehensive discipleship
means we learn how to bring all of life
under the leadership of Jesus.

WEEK
3

What Does it Mean to Be a Disciple of Jesus?

Introduction: We have seen that Jesus came to earth as God the Son for a purpose. He came to communicate God the Father's expectations for us and model how a life under his leadership should be lived. He also came to die for our sins so that we could reestablish a relationship with God. Embracing Jesus as our Savior and God allows us to begin the journey of becoming what God designed us to be while in relationship with him.

As we have seen, the Church is an assembly of believers living under the leadership of Jesus. We work together with our gifting to support one another and expand the kingdom. At this point, we need to understand the terminology Jesus used to describe his followers and what his relationship with his disciples looked like.

1. **Please read Appendix One, "The Meaning of *Mathētēs* (*Disciple*)."**

WEEK 3 - MEMORY VERSES
Luke 9:23, 6:40

2. **What did you learn about discipleship from the article?**

____

____

____

3. **From the article, how would you define a disciple of Jesus?**

____

____

____

4. **What three things did Wilkins say were true of a disciple in the culture at the time of Jesus?**

C ____

S ____

I ____

DISCIPLE OF JESUS

A disciple is someone who is a **committed follower** of Jesus, developing a **sustained relationship** with him in order to **imitate** him in all of life.

5. What do you think the words *discipleship* and *discipling* mean?

____

____

____

For our purposes, we will use the following definitions of ***disciple***, ***discipleship***, and ***discipling***:

Disciple of Jesus: describes someone who has

1. come to Jesus alone for eternal life,
2. embraced Jesus as Savior and God, and
3. embarked upon the life of following Jesus.[1]

Discipleship: living life with Jesus in order to become like him.

Discipling: helping others follow Jesus as his disciples.

At this point, it is important to see what Jesus said is involved in being his disciple.

6. How is the life of a disciple described in the following verses?

Committed Follower (Luke 9:23)

____

____

Sustained Relationship (John 15:9–11)

Imitation of Conduct (Galatians 4:19)

7. What do you think it means to take up your cross to follow Jesus?

8. How do the following quotes help clarify the meaning of taking up your cross?

> Theologian D. A. Carson states, "To take up your cross did not mean putting up with a toothache, job loss, or personal disability. Crucifixion was universally viewed as the most barbaric of Roman forms of execution, scarcely to be mentioned in polite company. The condemned criminal 'picked up his cross,' i.e., picked up the cross-member and carried it to the place of execution. If it was your lot to pick up your cross, there was no hope for you. There was only an . . . excruciating death."[2]

Theologians J. P. Moreland and Klaus Issler write, "Taking up our cross daily means to form the habit of going through our day with a certain orientation and attitude, namely, with a passion to give up our right to make ourselves the center of that day. Rather we live for God's kingdom, finding our place in his unfolding plan and playing our role well as we give our life away to others for Christ's sake."[3]

9. Where do you find it hard to apply this concept of dying to yourself?

____

____

10. What can we learn from Luke 6:40 in relation to discipleship?

____

____

11. What specifically have you been challenged with in this lesson and need to apply to your life?

____

____

____

____

WEEK
4

Jesus' Approach to Discipleship

Introduction: Now that we understand the terms *disciple*, *discipleship*, and *discipling*, it is important to see Jesus' method of discipleship with his followers. Discipleship was a common opportunity for those who lived in the time of Jesus. Many types of masters had disciples. Jesus took advantage of this common practice but altered it significantly to fit his purposes. In Jesus' day, many followed him and were even called disciples (John 6:66), but not all were true disciples. This study will seek to understand how Jesus did discipleship and how he distinguished between those who claimed to be disciples and those who really were his disciples.

1. **Read John 1:35–42. How would you describe STEP ONE in being a disciple of Jesus?**

___

___

WEEK 4 - MEMORY VERSES
Matthew 4:19

2. **Read Matthew 4:18–20 and Mark 1:16–18. What does STEP TWO look like?**

____

____

3. **What is the response to the command to follow in Matthew 4:19–20 and Matthew 19:21–22? Who is a true disciple?**

____

____

A proper response to the call of Jesus included three things:

- **Believing** in Jesus as the Messiah (John 2:11, 6:68–69)
- **Obeying** the request to follow (Mark 1:18, 20)
- **Personal Commitment** after counting the cost (Luke 14:25–33)

THE CALL

Jesus made a big change in his form of discipleship: responding to the command to follow or believe meant a person embraced Jesus as Savior and God after counting the cost and chose to follow him. At that point, he or she became his disciple.

4. **What does STEP THREE look like in John 6:1–65?**

____

____

5. **The fruit of the process of discipleship for Jesus is STEP FOUR. Read John 6:66–69 and describe what this last step looks like.**

____

____

In his very insightful book *Following the Master: A Biblical Theology of Discipleship,* Dr. Wilkins explains that Jesus had a clear process for following him. The following are insights from his study of the life of Jesus:

Stage One – Personal Initiative to Follow Jesus (John 1:35–42)

- People in that culture could take the initiative to follow a great master. Jesus allowed for this to be true with him as well.
- People followed Jesus out of curiosity, because they wanted to ask him questions and because they saw something in him that attracted them.

Stage Two – The Call of Jesus (Matthew 4:19; Mark 1:16)

- Jesus initiates the call. This was a challenge to believe in him as Savior and God. This was not done by other teachers.
- Those following Jesus were forced to make a life decision to either embrace Jesus and follow him or reject him. Faith is demonstrated by following.
- Those who believed came out of the crowd of followers and became true disciples.
- Luke 9:23 is an example of the cost expected if a follower wanted to become a disciple of Jesus.[1]

Wilkins explains, "Although entrance into the way of salvation and discipleship is found through faith alone . . . true faith meant having no allegiances that would hinder following after Jesus and carrying out the life of discipleship that would emanate. [2]

Stage Three – Jesus Sifts the Followers (John 6)

- Those following Jesus as his movement grew and consisted of "crowds" and "disciples" (see Mark 8:27–30, 34–38).
    - Jesus separates the two groups by teaching in parables and explaining the meaning to the disciples.
- He distinguishes the true disciples from the false with challenging teaching (John 6:14–69).
    - Feeding of five thousand (John 6:14–15)
    - Bread of Life (John 6:22–59)
    - The reaction (John 6:60)
    - Jesus' evaluation (John 6:64)
    - The departure (John 6:66)
    - True discipleship (John 6:67–69)

Stage Four – Limited Group of Followers

- True discipleship is for those who **believe** in Jesus as Savior and God, evidenced by having no **allegiance** before him, and is the result of a **personal commitment** to him after counting the cost of following him. Those who chose to leave after hearing his challenging teaching were not true disciples.

- The process of discipleship used by Jesus led to a reduced number of followers.[3]

6. **Have you seen people stop following Jesus? How do we explain that?**

____

____

7. **Read Matthew 13:3-8, 18-23. What can we learn from the way Jesus did ministry?**

____

____

8. **What do you think are the implications for us today as we help others follow Jesus?**

____

____

9. **Read Appendix Two, "An Incomplete Gospel." How would you summarize the problem addressed in that article?**

____

____

10. How are we to communicate a grace gospel while helping a person count the cost before he or she believes?

____

____

11. What stood out to you about discipleship in this lesson? What do you need to do differently to live as Jesus desires?

____

____

WEEK
5

THE MARKS OF A DISCIPLE OF JESUS

Introduction: What are the non-negotiable marks of a disciple of Jesus? This is an important question since we each desire to be clearly known as one of his disciples today. As we will see in this study, Jesus says there are three primary marks of his disciples.

MARK ONE OF A DISCIPLE OF JESUS

1. **Before we explore Jesus' teaching on this topic, what do you think are the non-negotiable evidences of a disciple of Jesus?**

____

____

____

____

WEEK 5 - MEMORY VERSES
John 8:31–32, 13:34–35, 15:8
(pick one)

2. **Read John 8:31–32. What is the MARK of a disciple in this passage?**

____

____

3. **What does it mean to "continue to follow my teaching" (see 2Timothy3:16–17)?**

____

____

- A disciple is someone who continually follows Jesus' teaching. He or she has a life yielded to the authority of Jesus as revealed in the Bible. The abundant life is the one lived under his leadership and according to his Word. As George R. Beasley-Murray explains, "The word ***abide*** or ***remain*** signifies a settled determination to live in the word of Christ and by it, and so entails a perpetual listening to it, reflection on it, holding fast to it, carrying out its bidding."[1]

THE WORD IS PROFITABLE FOR...

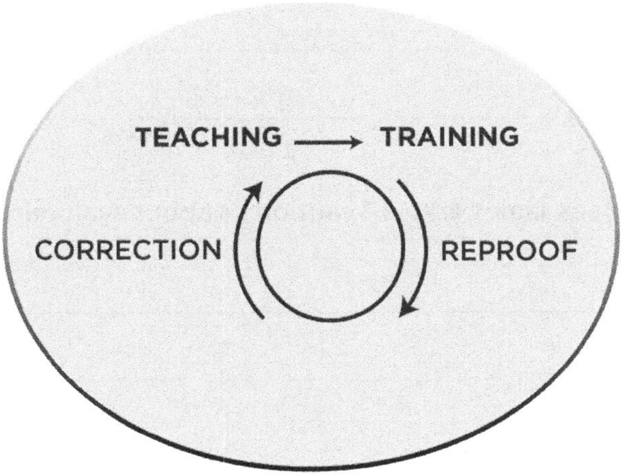

4. **How does the need to live by the Word relate to the way Jesus did discipleship from lesson four? In other words, why would he give this mark of a disciple?**

___

___

___

- Anyone could choose to follow Jesus. It was common for a person to pick a master to follow. Jesus allowed that but then called people to believe in him and his words. This call to believe was unique to his approach to discipleship. He gave clear teaching like this to sift those who followed so that true believers would be obvious.

- It is also important to remember that abiding in the Word is the process God uses to transform our minds (Romans 8:5–7, 12:1–2).

5. **What does this mean for those who claim to believe but are not living according to the Bible?**

___

___

6. **How does James 4:11–12 caution us about evaluating people?**

___

___

It is not our responsibility to judge the intent of the heart of others. We can only observe the fruit of the actions of others to discern if they give evidence of belief in Jesus.

7. **How does this expectation apply to you and me today?**

____

____

8. **Where do you struggle with the truth of John 8:31–32?**

____

____

____

____

Mark Two of a Disciple of Jesus

9. **Read John 13:34–35. What should be true of a disciple here?**

____

____

10. **What is new about this love?**

____

____

11. Read John 1:12 and see what insight it provides for the above question.

- Through faith in Christ, we become part of God's family. This means we are brothers and sisters, and love for family members is something new Jesus brings through faith in him.

- This love is also new because it has a new standard to be compared to. We are to love as Jesus loved. His sacrificial giving of himself for us is the new standard for our loving others.

12. What do you think loving other believers looks like (see Galatians 6:2, 10)?

____

____

13. Why is love so important for a disciple of Jesus (1 John 4:8)?

- Love describes the nature of God. Loving others shows the transformation of our hearts through God's work in us. It also reveals that our conduct imitates our Father.

Mark Three of a Disciple of Jesus

14. Read John 15:8. What do you see here that should be true of the disciple of Jesus?

____

____

15. Read Matthew 7:20 and Luke 6:43–44. What do these verses add to our understanding of John 15:8?

___

___

- Fruit gives evidence that a person is a disciple of Jesus. If there is fruit, it is obvious to all that a person is a disciple of Jesus.
- Fruit refers both to action and character in harmony with God's character.

16. What fruit should a disciple display (Galatians 5:22–23)?

___

___

17. The same word for fruit is used in Matthew 13:23. What is the point?

___

___

Fruit is that which naturally is produced from the plant. In our passage (John 15:8), Jesus is describing the way of life that comes from being connected to him. This way of life is the natural outflow of staying connected to him. This fruit is more fully explained in Galatians 5:22–23. It is the fruit of the Spirit's influence in us. It is the life that naturally flows as it is lived under the leadership of Jesus. It refers to character and action in harmony with God's expectations.

- Why is fruit important for a disciple of Jesus? Fruit that naturally flows from within is evidence of a transformed character.

Disciples with transformed characters live differently. Their character is like God's, and their actions are in harmony with God's desires.

THE MARKS OF A DISCIPLE

Jesus said three things give proof a person is his disciple: showing **love, abiding** in his Word, and bearing **fruit.**

18. What is one thing you have learned about following Jesus that you need to apply to your life?

WEEK
6

How Do We Become Like Jesus?

Introduction: Clear evidence of a disciple of Jesus includes showing love, abiding in Jesus and his Word, and bearing the fruit of a transformed character. These marks of a disciple should be progressively increasing in the life of a true follower of Jesus. The question we need to address in this lesson relates to how God works in us to change us so that bearing fruit, loving, and living in the truth are naturally flowing out of us.

1. **Read John 16:7–16 and Acts 1:8. What has the role of the Holy Spirit been since Jesus' return to the Father?**

   ____

   ____

   - The Holy Spirit, as the third person of the triune God, has a continued role in the world and in the lives of disciples of Jesus. (See the diagram on page 8.)

WEEK 6 - MEMORY VERSES
Ephesians 5:18

2. **Read 2 Corinthians 3:18 and Galatians 4:19. What specifically can the Holy Spirit do for the disciple?**

___

___

> ***THE HOLY SPIRIT***
> The Spirit is the one who is able to work in us to change us to be more like Jesus.

3. **Read Jeremiah 13:23 and Romans 7:21–24. Why do we need the Spirit?**

___

___

4. **Please read Appendix Three, "The Challenge of the Flesh." According to that article, why do we need the Holy Spirit?**

___

___

- Even believers have a fallen nature that is used to living apart from the will of God. This fallen nature does not go away when a person becomes a Christian. It is critical that the disciple understand how to be rightly related to the Spirit so that he can empower the disciple to say no to that fallen nature and live the way Jesus would desire.

5. **Read Romans 8:5, 9, 13–14. What is the hope for victory over sin in the life of the disciple?**

- Romans 8 reveals that the solution to the problem of our flesh is the Holy Spirit. As surely as Christ came to abolish the penalty of sin, the Spirit has come to indwell every believer for the purpose of continually conquering sin in the believer's experience.

- Sanctification describes the process by which a disciple progressively becomes like Jesus on earth as he or she is rightly related to the Spirit.

6. **Read 1 Corinthians 2:14–3:1. What three types of people do you see described there?**

7. **What is different or similar in the people mentioned in 1 Corinthians 2:14–3:1?**

There are three types of people mentioned in the passage above. The **"natural"** man is not a disciple of Jesus. The **"spiritual"** man is rightly related to the Holy Spirit so that his life can be changed. The **"worldly"** man is a disciple, but because he is not rightly related to the Holy Spirit, you cannot tell a difference in the fruit of his life from the "natural" man.

"The carnal man is the man who lives by the flesh, according to the dictates of the flesh, and the spiritual man is the man who lives by the power of the Spirit."[1]

8. How can the disciple become rightly related to the Spirit and live like the "spiritual" man?

____

____

____

____

There are four commands in the New Testament explaining how believers are to be rightly related to the Holy Spirit. The first two are negative, meaning they tell us what not to do:

Negative

- Ephesians 4:30 - *Do not grieve*

  This phrase is used in Matthew 26:22 and 1 Thessalonians 4:13. The term *grieve* describes deep sorrow. In the context, it refers to the pain and sorrow the Spirit feels when there is a lack of love and unity among believers.

- 1 Thessalonians 5:19 - *Do not quench or put out*

  Do not put out the Spirit as you would a fire. This in context is referring to suppressing the Word and saying no to God's will.

Both of these negative commands describe the fruit of sin in the life of a disciple. Sin impacts the Holy Spirit's ability to work in us, to empower us, to change us, and to enable us to live the life Jesus would desire.

9. **Read 1 Peter 3:18 and 1 John 1:9. How do these passages work together in the life of the disciple?**

   ____

   ____

   ____

   ____

For the disciple, there is a difference between a relationship with God and fellowship with God. When a person embraces Jesus as Savior and Lord, he or she becomes a disciple (Christian) and part of his family. The disciple's relationship with God will never change. A disciple will always be God's child.

Even though Jesus has judicially paid for all sin, the fruit of sin in the disciple has an impact on his or her fellowship with God. Sin hinders a person's ability to enjoy a relationship with God.

The way to address sin in the life of the disciple is through confession. Disciples need to admit their sin to God and tell him they are sorry. Then they need to ask for his forgiveness so that they can allow the Holy Spirit to continue his work.

Paul gives us two additional, positive commands in Galatians and Ephesians:

Positive

- Ephesians 5:18–20 – *Be filled with*

  If this command is done, then all other commands in relation to the Spirit will be fulfilled.

- Galatians 5:16 – *Walk in*

  This phrase refers to walking in the path of the Spirit as it is found in the Bible.

10. How are we to be filled with the Spirit?

- Being filled with the Holy Spirit is not something you need to strive to obtain, pray for, earn, etc. We all have the Spirit in us at the moment of salvation (Ephesians 1:13–14; 1 Corinthians 12:13; Romans 8:9).

BE FILLED

The context of this command reveals that the issue is one of control and influence. Paul's illustration is that, as wine influences a person and makes that person do what he or she would not normally do, so does the Spirit. The Spirit's control enables us to overcome the flesh and live rightly, which we could not do otherwise.

> Theologian J. Dwight Pentecost explains, "When the apostle talks about being filled with the Spirit, he proceeds to show that one who is under the control of, or the influence of, the Holy Spirit, will find that the controlling Holy Spirit produces an entirely different kind of life. The man is different, not because of what he is himself, but because of the power to which he has submitted himself and the Person to whom he has yielded control."[2]

The word in Ephesians used for *fill* is ***plēroō***. It is a word used to describe how the sails of a ship are filled by the wind. Sails are not just filled, but the ship is moved as a result of the filled sails. The Holy Spirit moves us and enables us to obey as we are filled by him (that is, as we are under his control). As the wind fills the sails of a ship and moves it to a specific course, so does the Spirit with our lives. When we yield to his leadership as found in his Word, we are filled.[3]

Summary:

1. **"Do not grieve" (Ephesians 4:30) and "Do not quench" (1 Thessalonians 5:19)**
    - Sin hinders the Spirit from working in and through the believer.

2. **Confess your sins and yield (1 John 1:9)**
    - Talk to God, admit your sin, and ask for his forgiveness.
    - If sin has been confessed, then the believer must yield to Christ's leadership (Romans 12:1-2; Luke 9:23).

3. **"Be filled with the Spirit" (Ephesians 5:18)**
    - Being filled with the Spirit does not automatically happen. This is a command in the passive voice

showing that the subject of the verb is to "let himself or herself be filled." We are to yield to the authority of the Word so the Spirit can fill us.

Theologian Eldon Woodcock writes, "What the Holy Spirit accomplishes within a believer depends on the extent to which the believer is yielded to the Spirit's influence. Since the extent of a believer's yieldedness varies, the extent of the Holy Spirit's control also varies. . . As a believer surrenders more control of his or her life to the Holy Spirit, that person experiences spiritual growth and progressive victory over sin. Therefore to maximize the Holy Spirit's influence, believers need to be completely open to His leading."[4]

- The believer, by faith in God's promises (Ephesians 5:18; 1 John 5:14–15), assumes he or she is Spirit filled when the first three steps are met.

4. "Walk in the Spirit" (Galatians 5:16)

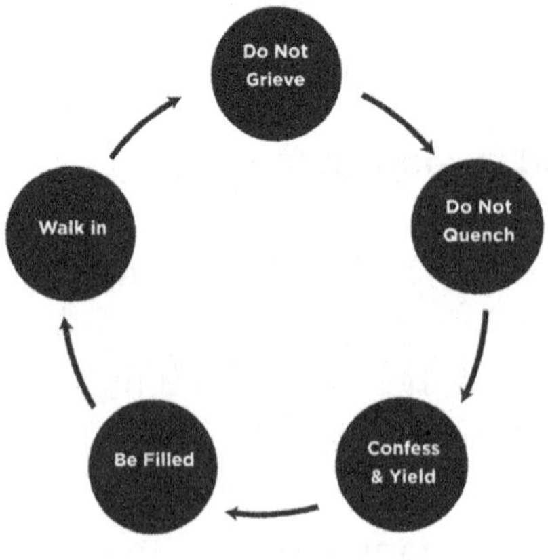

- As he or she is filled with the Spirit, the believer walks in the path of the Spirit as that path is revealed in Scripture.
- This continues until the believer grieves or quenches the Spirit through sin; then the process is repeated.

WEEK
7

NEW RELATIONSHIPS: LIVING AS FAMILY

Introduction: In the previous lesson we learned how the Holy Spirit works within us to change us into the image of Jesus over time as we yield to his leadership in our lives. This change is accomplished as we walk in the path of God's Word, confess our sins as they occur, and are empowered by the Holy Spirit as we submit to his control. Although this process is critical for our growth, God did not design us to pursue discipleship to Jesus alone. Instead, he made our spiritual growth a team effort. We need others in our lives to model the Christian life for us, to encourage us, and to support us. This lesson will explore these concepts in more detail.

1. **Read John 1:12. What new relationship do we share as disciples of Jesus?**

____

____

____

WEEK 7 - MEMORY VERSES
John 1:12

*"But as many as received Him to them He gave the right to **become children of God,** to those who believe in His name"* (John 1:12 NASB).

This verse gives us great news! Although we are all created by God, it is through our faith in Jesus as our Savior and God that allows us to become one of his children!

2. **If you and I are children of God through faith in Jesus, what does that make us?**

____

____

____

The truth that we are children of God through faith in Jesus means we are now part of a new family, God's family. Notice how early church scholar Dr. Hellerman describes this:

> "No image for the church occurs more often in the New Testament than the metaphor of **family.** References abound to believers as siblings (brothers and sisters) and to God as the 'Father' of His people."[1]

If disciples of Jesus are part of God's family, that means we are brothers and sisters! The New Testament writers used the descriptions ***brothers*** and ***sisters*** for believers because these terms were the closest relational terminology in their culture.[2]

3. What is the significance of our being in God's family?

___

___

___

We do not need to live the Christian life on our own! God wants us to work together as a family to follow him. As we work together expressing our gifting, we help each other grow in our relationship with Jesus, and we can become all that God designed us to be. Thus, we should make these Christian relationships a high priority in our lives.

4. How is our new family related to our discipleship to Jesus?

___

___

___

Although Jesus calls each of us individually to follow him, he designed this process to be done with those in our spiritual family. Dr. Issler says the following: "For Jesus, discipleship or disciple making primarily takes place **in the context of community.**"[3]

This concept is further explained by Dr. Wilkins when he says, "Jesus called **individuals to discipleship**, yet responding to that call brought disciples into a **community of faith**. . . . As Luke continues his story from the Gospel to the **book of Acts he allows us to see the crucial necessity of the community for discipleship**. . . . Through the Spirit, the community would now provide the fellowship, encouragement, edification and mutuality for following the Master in the new era."[4]

Discipleship to Jesus, then, requires both personal discipleship and family discipleship as is explained in the following diagram:

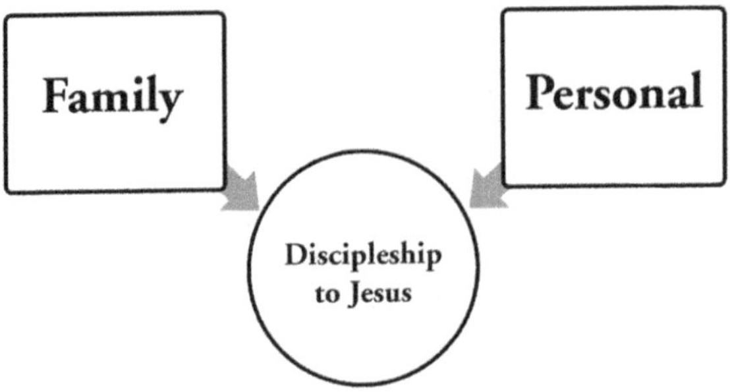

5. Why are family relationships with other Christians important?

Since we are relational beings, we need others in our lives. It is in the context of being relationally connected to others in which I can learn important relational truths that will help me grow. Dr. Hellerman helps to clarify how this works when he says, "Spiritual formation [becoming like Jesus] occurs primarily in the context of community [family]. People who remain connected with their brothers and sisters in the local church almost invariably grow in self-understanding, and they mature in their ability to relate in healthy ways to God and to their fellow human beings."[5]

6. Where is the best place to live out your new family relationships with other Christians?

The local church is often the best place to be part of a New Testament family.

7. **What would others see if the church family lived as brothers and sisters?**

____

____

____

The following chart shows some of what should happen in the ***church family*** and in our ***personal discipleship.***

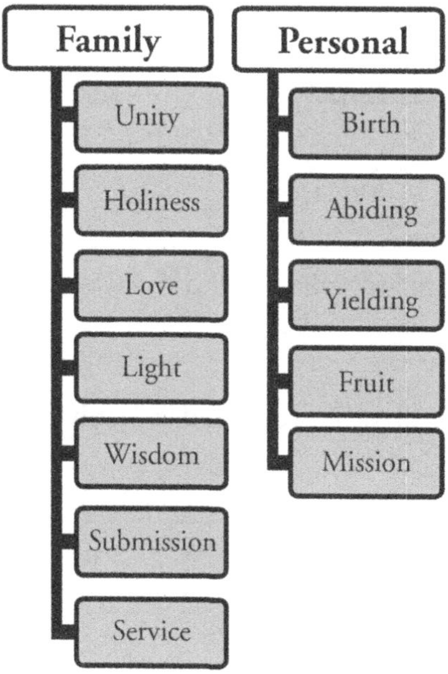

God's plan for our growth includes learning from others in relationships of trust. As a result, we are to put as much effort into our church family relationships as we do into our personal discipleship. It is in relationship to others that we learn how to live out our discipleship to Jesus.

This following diagram shows how our ***personal discipleship*** expresses itself in our ***church family relationships.***

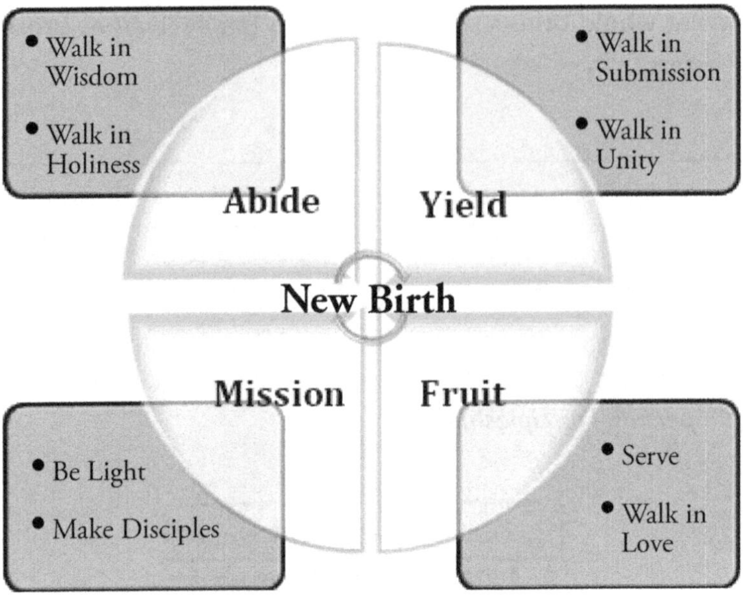

Our personal growth and discipleship to Jesus expresses itself in relationship to others in the church family and also to those outside the family.

8. What important truth is revealed in 1 John 3:14?

____

____

____

Notice how the NET Bible summarizes this verse: *"Our love for our fellow Christians is in fact* ***a form of*** *God's* ***love*** *for us because as far as the author of 1 John is concerned, all love comes from God."*

This verse is teaching us that God actually loves us through others! A very tangible way of experiencing God's love in your life is being relationally connected to other Christians.

9. What do you think others would think of the church if they saw us loving one another because we are now part of God's family?

____

____

Notice Dr. Hellerman's observation about this truth in the early church:

> "The early Christians intentionally organized their local congregations around the relational values [of family] . . . , **and these churches reproduced themselves and swept through the pagan empire of Rome like a holy fire.** Even pagan detractors identified fraternal love as something especially Christian: 'See,' Tertullian quotes the unbeliever as exclaiming, 'how they love one another!'"[6]

10. How do church family relationships thrive? Make your observations on the following verses:

Romans 15:7 ____________________________________

Colossians 3:16 __________________________________

Galatians 6:2 ___________________________________

Romans 14:19 ___________________________________

1 Corinthians 12:25 ________________________________

James 5:16 ______________________________

Romans 12:10 ______________________________

1 Thessalonians 4:18 ______________________________

11. What would it take from each of us to make the family experience work?

____

____

____

One of the first requirements would be that we make these family relationships a **priority** in our lives. Relationships with others do not just happen. They take time and work to help them flourish.

These relationships also will require from me that I **seek the interests of others above my own interests**. I need to learn that my participation in the lives of others is not primarily about me but rather about others. It is not about what I will get out of it but what I can do for others to help them grow in their relationship with Jesus. I need to be seeking to live out with others the "one another" passages we just looked at. If we all lived this way, all our needs would be met.

12. What do you need to do to become more connected to God's family?

____

____

____

WEEK
8

Developing Your Relationship with God

Introduction: The disciple of Jesus should seek to grow in his or her relationship with God. One key ingredient for enhancing this relationship is prayer. Prayer is the wonderful opportunity to talk to God, share your heart, and align with God with any requests we make. It is therefore very important to understand some basic concepts when we pray.

Notice what the following men said about prayer:

- Martin Luther is credited with saying, "I have so much to do today that I must spend the first three hours in prayer."
- Oswald Chambers said, "Prayer does not fit us for the greater works; prayer is the greater work."[1]

WEEK 8 - MEMORY VERSES
1 John 5:14–15

1. **What is it about prayer that would cause these great men to have such a high view of it?**

____

____

____

2. **How would you define prayer?**

____

____

____

- **Prayer** = "Human speech that is addressed toward God"[2]

3. **Why do we need to pray?**

____

____

____

- Prayer is a means of developing our relationship with God.
- Prayer is an expression of our dependence upon him and our need for his loving involvement in our lives.
- Prayer is our opportunity to express ourselves to God.
- Prayer allows us to be aligned with his will.

4. When we pray, what are some things we are assuming?

____

____

____

____

- God is omniscient.
- God is omnipotent.
- God is sovereign.
- God is love.
- God hears.
- God cares.

5. Are there limits to what prayer can achieve?

____

____

____

____

- As Christians, we can pray about whatever is on our hearts, but we can only expect answers in relation to the limits Scripture places upon prayer.

The First Limit to Prayer – Mark 11:20-24

6. What does Mark 11:20-24 mean?

____

____

____

- Faith is not the mere belief that something will happen. Faith always has an object and content. The object of our faith is found in verse 22. It is God. The content of faith is always the promise of God.

- Faith is believing God will do what he promises!

- As Dr. Wayne R. Spear says, "Faith is not the belief that 'anything can happen,' but the confidence that what God has promised will happen. In accordance with this, the content of the prayer of faith is determined by what God has promised."[3]

- This passage does not teach that the answer of prayer is dependent upon the one praying. The emphasis of this passage is on God's ability to do as he promised.

- Dr. Spear clarifies that "Mark 11:24, then, does not contain an unlimited promise that any prayer will be answered. The promise is qualified by faith, and faith is seen here to rest upon what has been revealed of God's nature and promise."[4]

- **Prayer limited by faith** does not mean that our prayer is based upon our ability to believe something will happen but that our prayer is limited to the specific promises of God. Faith always rests in God and relies on the promise of God. Therefore, if God has not specifically promised it, then no amount of belief or praying will make it happen. The prayer of faith is simply trusting God to do as he promised.

> ***MOVING MOUNTAINS***
>
> Moving mountains was a common Jewish expression. It was a reference to removing difficulties.
>
> As a result, prayer is the means God has given us to address all problems and help us deal with all difficulties.

The Second Limit to Prayer— 1 John 5:14–15

7. **What do you think 1 John 5:14–15 means?**

____

____

____

Prayer that is limited by God's will means that prayer is in harmony with God's revealed will—Scripture. Such prayer relates to specific promises and commands God has given to the church.

- Donald Burdick explains, "The knowledge that what we ask for agrees with God's will can best be derived from God's Word. If our request is in accord with God's revealed will, we may be sure of a favorable hearing. It is not enough to feel that it is in harmony with the divine will. Such subjective confidence may well be completely without foundation in fact. Nor can we force God to adjust to our will. Instead, we are to adjust our desires and petitions to His will."[5]

- John Stott further clarifies that "prayer is not a convenient device for imposing our will upon God, or for bending his will to ours, but the prescribed way of subordinating our will to his. It is by prayer that we seek God's will, embrace it and align ourselves with it."[6]

The Third Limit to Prayer — John 14:13–14

8. What do you think John 14:13–14 means?

____

____

____

Praying in the name of Jesus is not some magical formula tacked on to the end of our prayers to ensure God will answer them. It is an admission that **what is prayed for is within the revealed will and purpose of Christ**. Such prayer is **in harmony with his plan and will as it is found in Scripture**.

- Dr. Spear expounds upon Jesus' words: "Thus in John 14:3, 'whatever you ask' is not unrestricted, but is governed by the phrase, 'in my name.' The promise of an answer is given only to prayer which is in harmony with the revelation which centers in Christ. Again, the content of prayer is regulated by the Word of God."[7]

- Prayer is to be prayed in the name of Jesus. This is an admission that such prayer is in harmony with his revealed will and purpose as it is contained within Scripture.

- "A person's name in the ancient world represented what the person was like."[8]

9. In this first lesson on prayer, what most stood out to you?

____

____

____

> ***Pray as though everything depended on God; work as though everything depended on you.***
>
> ***— Augustine***[9]

10. In light of our study on prayer today, what needs to change in your prayer life?

____

____

____

E. M. Bounds writes, "Prayer honors God, acknowledges His being, exalts His power, adores His providence, and secures His aid."[10]

WEEK
9

Praying with Confidence

Last week, we saw that biblical prayer is limited in three ways. Our prayers need to be offered in faith, in harmony with the will of God, and, finally, in the name of Jesus.

For prayer requests to have the guaranteed answer of yes, they must be based upon a promise of God's Word, and according to God's revealed will within Scripture. They must also be asked for in the name of Jesus, showing that they are in harmony with his revealed plan and purpose as contained in Scripture.

> ***PRAYER***
>
> Prayer is primarily designed for us to talk to God about what is on his heart. In this way, we further his kingdom and align ourselves with his will.

What hits you about the following quotes?

- E. M. Bounds explains, "A prayerless age will have but scant models of divine power."[1]

WEEK 9 - MEMORY VERSES
Luke 22:42

- Andrew Murray states, "Prayer is the pulse of life; by it the doctor can tell what is the condition of the heart."[2]

If prayer needs to be in line with God's will, how can we pray with confidence if we are not sure what is God's will? In this lesson, we will look at **three types of petition** in the Bible. Once we understand these types of petition, then we need to learn how we are to practically apply these truths to our lives so we can pray biblically and confidently.

1. **Read James 4:3. What would you name the FIRST TYPE of prayer request? What can we learn from this?**

- The people to whom James was writing were praying with the wrong motives. They were using prayer for self-gratification. Obviously, such prayer is a waste of one's time because God is not interested in selfish prayer that is contradictory to his Word.

2. **Read 1 John 5:14–15. What would you name the SECOND TYPE of prayer request? What can we learn from this?**

- The second type of prayer request is prayer in harmony with God's will.

As John Calvin said, "Again, only out of faith is God pleased to be called upon, and he expressly bids that prayers be conformed to the measure of his Word. Finally, faith grounded upon the Word is the mother of right prayer; hence as soon as it is deflected from the Word, prayer must needs be corrupted.[3]

3. How do we know if something is God's will for us today?

____

____

- Obviously, it is important for us to make a distinction between God's specific will for others and his timeless will for all of us. An example would be God's promise to make Abraham a great nation in Genesis 12. That was for Abraham, not us today. It would do no good to pray for the fulfillment of that promise today because God was not talking to us!

4. Read 2 Chronicles 20:2–13. Try to make an outline of Jehoshaphat's prayer. What model for prayer does Jehoshaphat leave us?

____

____

5. What is an example of a timeless promise you know of in the Bible that applies to you and me today and that God will answer?

____

____

6. Read Romans 1:10–13 and 2 Corinthians 12:7–9. What would you name the THIRD TYPE of petition?

___

___

- The third type of petition is prayer that seems to be a good idea to us and fits God's known revealed will, but we are not sure if it is what God wants.

7. How much of our prayer life today fits into this third category?

___

___

- Although most prayer should be the second type of prayer already discussed, for most of us, the majority of our prayer falls into this last category.

8. Read James 4:13–15 and Luke 22:41–45. How do these verses show that we should pray for this third type of request?

___

___

- Since we do not know for sure what God's will is if it is not stated in Scripture, we should be prayerfully active but humbly submissive to God's will. We should pray our hearts out about these requests, but in the end, we should tell God we want his will, not ours. Why? Because only he knows what is best.

9. Practically, how do we pray for this third type of request?

____

____

____

____

We need to pray and express our desires, knowing that we do not know what is best. We need to ask for God's will to be done, not ours. An example of praying this way would be how I prayed when my father had heart surgery:

- I prayed earnestly about this issue. I specifically asked God to protect and heal my dad. I asked that God would give the surgeons a good night's sleep so that they would be alert in surgery. I also prayed that God would guide the hands of the surgeons so that they would be able to complete the surgery successfully.

- Since no specific Scripture was related to my father's surgery, I appealed to the very character of God in my prayers. I praised him for his greatness, power, omniscience, and love. I reminded him of all of these things in relation to my father.

- I concluded with finally asking God to accomplish his will in this situation, for he is the one who knows best and loves my father more than I do. As a result of praying this way, I was confident of God's love for me and my father. I left confident that his will would be best even if it meant my father might die.

10. What if you have a hard time letting go and trusting God to accomplish his will instead of yours? What does 1 Peter 5:7 tell us we need to do?

____

____

11. Can you throw something if you do not let go of it?

____

____

- If you can't let go, it is evidence of a lack of faith in God's character.
- If you can't submit your heart to God's will in relation to this type of request, you are not praying the way he wants you to pray. Instead of allowing prayer to conform you to his will, you are using prayer as a way to make God do things the way you want them done.
- If you cannot honestly say that you desire God's will in such a request, go back on your knees until you can.

The following chart summarizes what we have learned about praying with confidence. The Bible is the foundation for prayer.

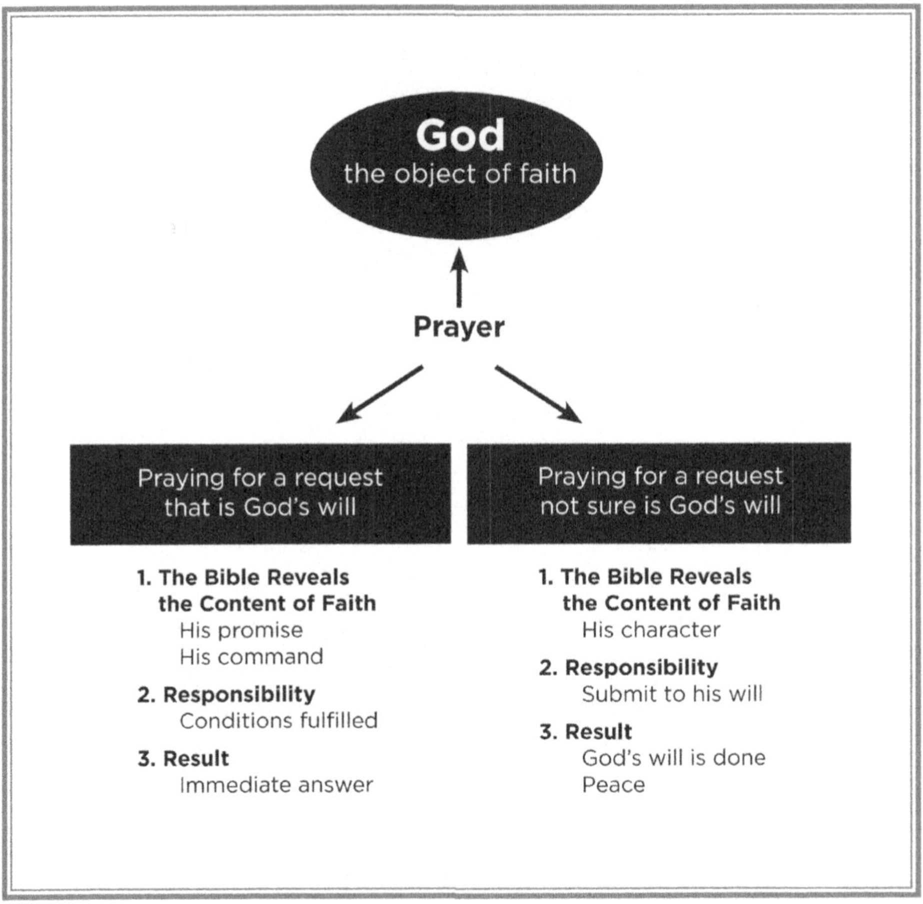

12. In light of our study of prayer, what do you need to do differently in your prayer life?

___

___

___

WEEK 10

Living by Faith Rather Than Feelings

Introduction: What does the normal Christian life look like? How do our feelings relate to our obedience? What should we do if we do not feel close to God or do not feel like living a life of faithfulness?

1. **What would our lives as disciples look like if we lived by our feelings—if we let those feelings determine our actions in the Christian life?**

____

____

____

2. **Read Hebrews 11. What stands out to you in that chapter?**

____

____

WEEK 10 - MEMORY VERSES
Hebrews 11:6

3. **How would you define faith?**

___

___

- **Faith** = reliant trust in God to accomplish his promises.

> ### *BIBLICAL FAITH*
> It is important to understand that biblical faith always has an object and content. The object of our faith is God. The content of our faith is his promises as they are found in his Word.

4. **If faith is reliantly trusting in God to accomplish his promises, how would you define living by faith?**

___

___

- **Living by faith** = choosing to believe that God is trustworthy and acting as though his promises are true, regardless of our feelings at the moment.

A simple way to remember this truth is this phrase:
"*Faith it until you feel it.*"

5. **What must we firmly believe if we use that definition of living by faith?**

____

____

To be able to live by faith, we must be convinced of God's character and reliability and the truth of his Word. If we doubt these things, we will struggle in following him, and we could end up allowing our feelings to guide our path instead of simple faith in God and his promises.

6. **Are you living as though you believe God and his promises are true? Where do you struggle?**

____

____

7. **How do Numbers 23:19, 2 Timothy 3:16–17, and 2 Peter 1:20–21 relate to living by faith?**

____

____

____

____

8. **Please read Appendix Four, "The Most Unique Book Ever Written," and record what impacted you.**

____

____

____

____

____

____

____

9. **Read the following verses. What do they teach about the God we trust? Psalm 90:2**

____

____

Isaiah 40:13–14 ______________________________

____

Joshua 24:19; Psalm 99:3; Isaiah 40:25______________

____

Malachi 3:6; James 1:17 ________________________

____

1 Kings 8:27 __________________________________

____

1 John 4:8 ___________________________________

____

Genesis 17:1 ____

____

Psalm 139:7–11 ____

____

Psalm 139:16 ____

____

Psalm 11:7 ____

____

John 4:24 ____

____

John 17:3____

____

10. Where are you presently struggling with living by faith? Explain.

____

____

____

____

____

____

11. How does the diagram below help you understand living by faith?

____

____

____

____

1

I must choose to put my trust (faith) in God and his promises (fact) and let my feelings catch up. I cannot pull the train (my life) by my feelings.

12. What most impacted you in this lesson related to living by faith rather than by your feelings?

____

____

____

____

WEEK
11

Reading the Word to Change

Introduction: God has given us a handbook for life in the Bible. This book was given to us not just to provide information about God and his expectations of us but to change us. Hebrews 4:12 tells us that the Bible is "living and active." The Bible is able to pierce our hearts. It is God's Word that the Spirit uses to convict us, guide us, and change us. What is our responsibility to cooperate with the Holy Spirit and his Word so that change happens?

1. **How do we let the Word change us rather than simply give us knowledge?**

____

____

____

WEEK 11 - MEMORY VERSES
Colossians 3:16

2. **What do the following verses say about the Word's role in our life as disciples of Jesus?**

   Colossians 3:16

   ____

   2 Timothy 3:16–17

   ____

   2 Timothy 2:15

   ____

3. **How can we go from head knowledge of the Bible to heart knowledge that guides us in daily life?**

   ____

   ____

   ____

   ____

4. **Why is it so hard to live out the facts of the Bible?**

   ____

   ____

   ____

   ____

In *Exposition of Philippians*, William Hendriksen and Simon J. Kistemaker explain, "True believers **hear** [the Word]. They **meditate** until they understand. Then they **act** upon it, putting it into constant practice, thereby showing that their house was built upon a rock."[1]

Notice the following diagram that helps us understand the process of moving from head knowledge to heart knowledge.

When we approach the Bible:

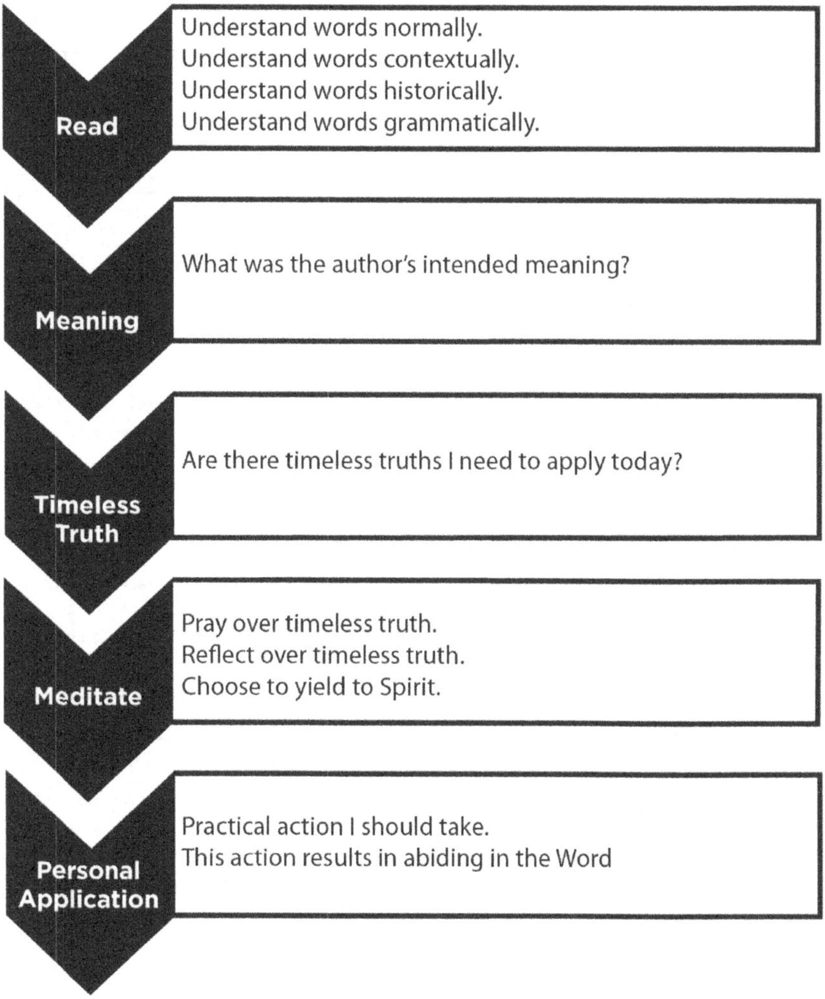
Read
Understand words normally.
Understand words contextually.
Understand words historically.
Understand words grammatically.
Meaning
What was the author's intended meaning?
Timeless Truth
Are there timeless truths I need to apply today?
Meditate
Pray over timeless truth.
Reflect over timeless truth.
Choose to yield to Spirit.
Personal Application
Practical action I should take.
This action results in abiding in the Word

5. **How far do you normally get in the previous chart when reading the Bible?**

6. **What do you not understand about this process?**

7. **What are some common reasons you may not get through this process when you read the Bible?**

The following diagram explains the meditation step in more detail:

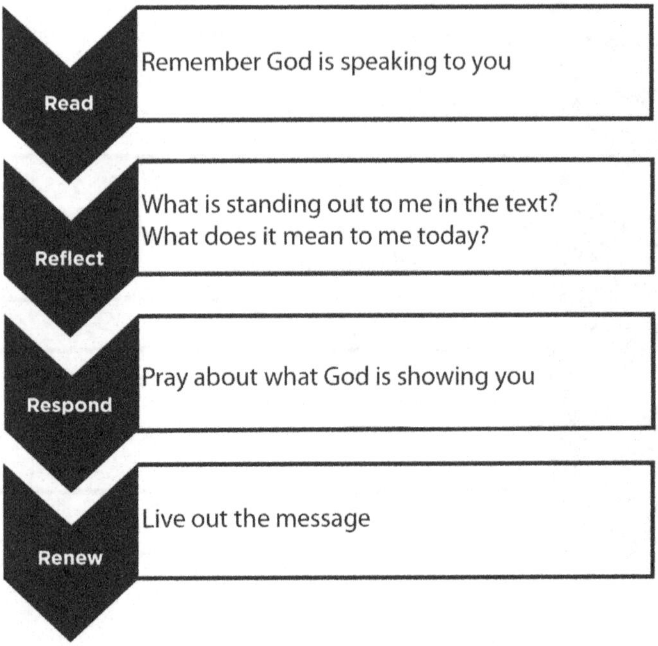

8. **What have you learned from this simple process?**

9. **How will this impact the way you read the Bible in the future?**

10. **Who will you take through this discipleship study?**

APPENDIX ONE

THE MEANING OF MATHĒTĒS (DISCIPLE)

There are a number of reasons why discipleship seems to be a struggle for church participants, including those in a multi-site setting. The first seems to revolve around the various understandings of the meaning of the word ***mathētēs*** (***disciple***) and what discipleship to Jesus looks like in everyday life. If we are not clear about the meaning of the word ***mathētēs***, then we will not be able to evaluate if a person is able to accomplish discipleship.

Today it seems common for well-respected teachers to define the word ***disciple*** as "learner," which unfortunately misses the depth of meaning the word had in Jesus' time.

We can see an example of that simplified definition from a popular teacher here:

> The Greek word translated as disciple comes from a verb that means "to learn." A ***disciple*** attached himself to another to gain practical or theological knowledge by instructions or experience. It was a word used of apprentices learning a trade as well as students learning a teacher's philosophy.[1]

Promoting the meaning of ***mathētēs*** primarily as "learner" leads to a pupil/teacher relationship. This understanding of the meaning of discipleship then results in an approach that is primarily informational and could be reduced to a class you graduate from rather than a life lived in relationship with Jesus. If discipleship is primarily informational, it is also understandable why some might choose not to participate. This approach could inadvertently lead to the idea that discipleship is only for the committed people, those willing to pay the price to gain the knowledge required for discipleship, rather than an understanding that discipleship is for all believers and is expected of all believers. Teaching that the meaning of ***mathētēs*** is simply "learner" misses the fuller meaning of the word Jesus employed to describe his followers and will negatively impact discipleship efforts in the church if adopted.

This limited view of the meaning of ***mathētēs*** also completely misses the transformation expected of a disciple of Jesus. This internal transformation comes from living in a vibrant, personal relationship with Jesus while being under his leadership. Over time, the disciple grows to love Jesus and should be changed to look more like him as his or her character reflects the character of God. This type of transformation is not intended to be optional in Christ's approach to discipleship but should be the natural fruit of walking with him according to his Word. The goal of discipleship is not information and participation in church events or programs but transformation over time as we walk in fellowship with Jesus so that we become like him in all of life.

Dr. Michael J. Wilkins gives valuable insight as to the fuller meaning of the word mathētēs when he states, "A *mathētēs* was a **committed follower** of a great master, although the type of master ranged from philosopher to great thinker-master of the past to religious figures. The commitment assumed the development of a **sustained relationship** between the follower and the master, and the relationship extended to the **imitation of the conduct** of the master."[2]

Wilkins's observation shows us that the term ***mathētēs*** takes learning from Jesus to a much deeper level: we disciples follow after him for our entire lives, enjoying a "sustained relationship" with him and, as a result, learning to do what he expects in all areas of our lives. All of these ingredients must be promoted in the concept of discipleship from the very beginning of the presentation of the gospel. Discipleship involves not only gaining information but also being transformed over time into Christlikeness as we live in relationship to him.

Although learning and following are parts of the history of the meaning of the word ***mathētēs*** and are important to the discipleship process, people must be taught that being a disciple of Jesus is much broader than that. As Wilkins states, "In the specific sense, a disciple of Jesus is one who has come to Jesus for eternal life, has claimed Jesus as Savior and God, and has embarked upon the life of following Jesus."[3]

Discipleship to Jesus includes embracing the life of following him with the goal of becoming like him in every area of life. Being a disciple of Jesus, then, means having a relationship with Jesus that is practical for everyday living and results in the reproduction of that life and faith in others.

As a result of these clarifications, we can see that discipleship to Jesus is for everyone who has come to him as their Savior and God. Following Jesus is not for a select, committed few. Discipleship is for all believers.

All Christians are called to be in the process of becoming like their Master—Jesus. Every believer also has the responsibility of passing on his or her faith to others (see Matthew 28:18–20). Each believer should be in discipleship to Jesus and intentionally be in the process of helping others do the same.

Discipleship to Jesus and the new life we have in relationship to him allows us to become all that God has designed us to be. Wilkins notes that this restored relational connection to God allows a person to be more complete, whole, healthy, fulfilled, and effective in every area of life.[4]

Discipleship to Jesus, then, is the heart and soul of what the church should be pursuing both individually and as a group.

Unfortunately, recent research shows that the average church attendee does not understand the importance of this concept. In George Barna's view, the primary barrier to effective discipleship is "not that people do not have the ability to become spiritually mature, but they lack the passion, perspective, priorities, and perseverance to develop their spiritual life."[5]

The church today must realize its responsibility to help all believers embrace the privilege and responsibility of being a disciple of Jesus in all of life. This is what the church is designed to be.

APPENDIX TWO

AN INCOMPLETE GOSPEL

Somehow, possibly in our concern not to proclaim a works gospel, the church has managed to proclaim a gospel that seems to allow a person to choose to embrace Christ as Savior without the expectation of that person following Jesus and becoming like him over time.

In contrast to this limited view of the gospel, Dietrich Bonhoeffer states, "When Christ calls a man, he bids him come and die."[1] Bonhoeffer understood that Christianity was not designed to be lived on the disciples' terms but on Christ's terms: the gospel is to be offered graciously and without charge, but to embrace it will cost a person's life. Following Jesus as a disciple should be expected and is the normal outflow ofthe choice to believe in Jesus as Savior and God. **"Believe" is how the gospel of forgiveness and life is received, but "follow" is how the life of a disciple is to be lived.** The Christian must believe in Jesus as Savior and God for the forgiveness of his or her sins and for new life, but that new life is expected to be lived by following Jesus on his terms.

Keith Matthews summarizes the current state of the incomplete gospel well when he says the following:

> It seems to me that we have substituted a reduced gospel that focuses solely on "forgiveness of sins and the assurance of salvation" as our present gospel appeal. But here's the most obvious problem: This conversion-centered approach to the gospel has for many people been interpreted as a finish line or an ending, instead of a starting line or new beginning. This understanding has huge implications for how we live life now! If being forgiven and now having heaven assured is what it means to become a Christian, anything I do from there on is an add-on. "Why talk to me about discipleship? Why do I need that?

I've been forgiven. I'm already going to heaven. What more do I need to do?"[2]

Matthews explains the problem well when he notes that many Christians view salvation as a finish line rather than the starting line. The church must be careful to explain not just the free gift of forgiveness but the expectation of embracing the life of following the Master as well in the call to discipleship.

For those who followed him, Jesus' form of discipleship included his call to believe.[3] Following Jesus was evidence of their choice to believe in him (see John 1:43; Mark 1:17, 2:1; and Matthew 19:21 for examples). Wilkins also clarifies that disciples separated themselves from the crowd following Jesus by their choice to believe and acknowledge Jesus as Lord.[4]

This call of Jesus forced a person to respond in faith and obedience or leave him (see John 6:22–66). Not only must the gospel call to discipleship be clear but also it must be done in a way that allows people to understand how to apply it to their lives. Until the gospel is clarified, as John Stott states, the fruit of this incomplete gospel is that "superficiality is everywhere."[5]

This call and need to follow Jesus on his terms is clearly communicated when Jesus says, "If anyone would come after me, let him deny himself and take up his cross daily and follow me" (Luke 9:23 ESV). This challenge of Jesus is describing both the initial call to believe, which includes counting the cost of following Jesus before salvation, and the daily expectation of a disciple of the Master. All three requirements in Luke 9:23 are commands. **The daily choice of the disciple is deciding who he or she is going to live for.** The disciple's choice will affect his or her fellowship with Jesus, power for living, and the fruit of his or her ministry. When we let others know they can be disciples of Jesus, we must clearly explain the expectation of following Jesus. Potential disciples must know that salvation is still by grace and through faith, but the cost of salvation is their life as their will is yielded to Jesus in discipleship to him.

As J.P. Moreland and Klaus Issler state, "For a disciple of Jesus, to take up our cross daily means to form the habit of going through our day with a certain orientation and attitude, namely, with a passion to give up our right to make ourselves the center of that day. Rather, we live for God's kingdom, finding our place in His unfolding plan and playing our role well as we give our life away to others for Christ's sake."[6]

Discipleship to Jesus must also be presented in such a way that it is about Jesus and our relationship with him. In the life of discipleship, one of the important things the disciple learns is how to live for Jesus rather than himself.

These expectations must be communicated to a person when he or she comes to Christ for salvation. Matthew Henry believed that self-denial was the key to following Jesus. He felt that it was the first step in the life of following Jesus. It was this step that would allow a person to enjoy all the benefits that come with a relationship with Jesus.[7]

As we walk in this type of relationship with Jesus and under his leadership, we can expect to experience a love relationship with him. Jesus said it this way: "As the Father has loved me, so have I loved you. Abide in my love. If you keep my commandments, you will abide in my love, just as I have kept my Father's commandments and abide in his love. These things I have spoken to you, that my joy may be in you, and that your joy may be full" (John 15:9–11 ESV).

In addition to enjoying a relationship with Jesus and following him on his terms, the disciple can also expect to be conformed to him over time. Paul communicates this truth: "Oh, my dear children! I feel as if I am going through labor pains for you again, and they will continue until Christ is fully developed in your lives" (Galatians 4:19 NLT). Paul longed to see Christlikeness in his disciples.

A student of mine made a great observation about life change. She said, "I feel like a chocolate chip cookie. The cookie is my life and the chocolate chips are the Christian aspects that I have chosen to add to my recipe called 'Mitzi': a little Bible study here, some community group there, a dash of ShareFest [service project], a quiet time occasionally, and so on—you get the idea. Now, what do I really want to be? A dense, rich chocolate brownie, where the chocolate, or Christian life, is so intermingled and minute by minute part of my life that you can't see where the chocolate ends and the rest of the batter begins. I want to be a glimpse of Christ's invisible character on earth."[8]

This illustration shows that our lives are supposed to change as a result of following Jesus. The disciple of Jesus' character should be molded and transformed over time, and he or she should also help others experience the same. Wilkins believes that the marks of a disciple of Jesus will include the fruit of the Spirit displayed in the life of the believer, outreach so that others come to know Jesus, as well as a righteous life with good works others can observe.[9]

Discipleship to Jesus, then, includes far more than the initial choice to believe in him as Savior and God. It also includes the life of following his ways so that we might be changed over time to become more like him. **Life for the disciple of Jesus is a life lived for him, in a vital relationship with him, so that we might become like him.**

APPENDIX THREE

THE CHALLENGE OF THE FLESH

WHAT IS THE FLESH?

Flesh (*sárx*) can mean "physical body," but in some cases, it takes on a figurative meaning with a spiritual emphasis. Paul describes this meaning in Romans 7. There Paul discusses the internal struggle all Christians experience (notice present tense and first person verbs. See also Philippians 3:4 for Paul's view of his life as a Jew).

- Romans 7:14 - The flesh is enslaved to sin. The verb tense is perfect, indicating past action (the fall) with present results.
- Romans 7:18 - There is no spiritual good in the flesh.
- Romans 8:3 - The flesh limits our efforts to obey.
- Galatians 5:17 - The flesh resists the spirit.
- Romans 7:21 - The "principle" (*nómos*) is described. This is the word for ***law***.

Just as there are physical laws that cannot be changed, so are there spiritual laws that cannot be changed. William Barclay describes Paul's struggle with these laws:

> PAUL is baring his very soul; and he is telling us of an experience which is of the very essence of the human situation. He knew what was right and wanted to do it; and yet, somehow, he never could. He knew what was wrong and the last thing he wanted was to do it; and yet, somehow, he did. He felt himself to be a split personality. It was as if two men were inside the one skin, pulling in different directions. He was haunted by this feeling of frustration, his ability to see what was good and his inability to do it; his ability to recognize what

was wrong and his inability to refrain from doing it.[1]

So what is the flesh?

The flesh is our inherited desire from Adam that makes us want to please ourselves instead of God.

How is the flesh at work in us?

- Romans 7:5 - It is aroused to rebel when exposed to the commands or will of God.
- Ephesians 2:1–3 - It is aroused to fulfill its lusts through exposure to the world system.

The flesh is aroused to rebel against God's will once it is aware of it or to fulfill its own selfish desires once it is tempted by the old world system. As a result, the fleshly principle in us is aroused to rebel all the time! The flesh is a big bully in us who is used to having its own way anytime it wants something.

How does the flesh work in us?

The word in both uses above is ***energéō***. It means literally "in" (***en***) + "work" (***ergon***). From this word we derive our English word ***energize*** ("to give energy to"). The flesh is energized to act when tempted to rebel or fulfil its own desires.

This law of the existence of the flesh also includes the principle that the flesh is more powerful than our will to do good. Even when I battle my flesh with all my good intentions, I am like a ninety-eight-pound weakling taking on a heavyweight boxing champion. I don't have a chance.

As we will see in our lesson, the Holy Spirit, the helper Jesus gave us, is our only hope to be able to overcome our natural desire to please ourselves instead of God.

APPENDIX FOUR

The Most Unique Book Ever Written

The Bible Stands Out

Here are some of the ways in which the Bible is unique.

A) Authorship

The Bible was written by forty different authors, including kings, shepherds, fishermen, and a tax collector. Not only did these authors come from varying social backgrounds but also the endless topics covered in Scripture (from theological to political) were written about by these authors without contradiction.

James Emery White observes that the Bible was "written in different places—from the wilderness, to a comfortable room, to a dungeon; written at different times—from war to peace; written during author's different moods—from the height of joy to the depths of despair; written on three continents—Asia, Africa and Europe; written in three languages—Hebrew, Aramaic and Greek; written concerning hundreds of controversial issues."[1]

B) Time span

The Bible was written over a 1,500-year span. The Old Testament is thought to have been started by Moses beginning in approximately 1446 BC at the time of the Exodus. The last New Testament letter was written by the apostle John around AD 95.

C) Preservation

Dr. Ken Boa and Larry Moody describe the endurance of the Bible:

> The Scriptures have survived through time, persecution, and criticism. There have been numerous attempts to burn, ban, and systematically eliminate the Bible; but all have failed. . . . The Bible has been subjected to more abuse, perversion, destructive criticism, and pure hate than any other book. Yet it continues to stand the test of time while its critics are refuted and forgotten. No other book has enjoyed such popularity—the Bible has been copied and circulated more extensively than any other book in human history. It has been translated into more languages than any other literature as well (portions now exist in more than 1,700 languages).[2]

D) Prophecy

Scripture is the only book in all the world that can say it accurately predicted the future without error.

In his book ***Evidence that Demands a Verdict***, Josh McDowell mentions mathematician Peter Stoner, who gave the probability of one person—Jesus—being able to fulfill the eight prophecies completely out of his control: place of birth, time of birth, manner of birth, betrayal, manner of death, people's reactions, his piercing, and his burial. Stoner observes the following:

> We find the chance that any man might have lived down to the present time and fulfilled all eight prophecies is 1 in 10 to the 17th (10 to the 17th power). That would be 1 in 100,000,000,000,000,000 (17 zeros after the one). In order to comprehend this staggering probability, Stoner illustrates it by supposing that we take 10 to the 17th silver dollars and lay them on the face of Texas. They will cover all of the state two feet deep. Now mark one of these silver dollars and stir the whole mass thoroughly, all over the state. Blindfold a man and tell him that he can travel as far as he wishes, but he must pick up one silver dollar and say that this is the right one. What chance would he have of getting the right one? Just the same chance that the prophets would have had of writing these eight prophecies and having them all come true in any one man.[3]

E) Beneficial effects of the Bible

The Bible has produced positive changes in the lives of millions of people. A transformed life is the fruit of belief in God's written word. A person's experience of the benefits of Scripture does not prove that the Bible is God's Word, but it does give additional evidence to consider in relation to its value. As Norman L. Geisler and Ronald M. Brooks state, "Any writing that does not exhibit the transforming power of God in the lives of its readers is not from God. 'For the Word of God is living and active and sharper than any two-edged sword' (Hebrews 4:12)."[4]

Why Did Jesus Come?

Purpose - The purpose of this first lesson is to introduce the gospel in a clear and fresh way. The hope is that this lesson will either clarify the gospel so that participants can become disciples of Jesus or confirm the choice participants have already made to believe in Jesus Christ as Savior and God.

Insights for Each Question

1. ***"In the beginning"*** – This is a reference to Genesis 1:1. It shows that Jesus was not created but was there at creation.

   "Was with God" – The preposition ***with*** means a "face to face relationship." It is stressing that the Word had an eternal relationship with the Father.

   "The Word was God" – This is a clear declaration of the deity of the Word.

2. Jesus communicated the Father to us. In other words, in many ways, Jesus has shown us what God is like through his teaching and his actions.

3. Read the information in the lesson to clarify the meaning of the title "Word" used of Jesus. Because Jesus is the Word, he expresses God's thoughts to us through his words and actions.

4. John shows us that the Word, God the Son, took on flesh to live among us and to accomplish his mission. Hebrews

2 shows why Jesus took on flesh so that he could take on humanity: it was only as the God-Man that he could die for our sins.

5. Jesus came to give us life. The fact that Jesus came to give us this life means we did not have it until he came.

6. It is helpful to see that Jesus used a special word for ***life*** to describe why he came to earth. Read the lesson to better understand the significance of this word.

7. John 1 – Jesus possesses this life.

   John 3 – This life is eternal. Jesus came to give others this life, which is available to those who believe in him.

   John 5 – Receiving this life moves a person from spiritual death to spritual life.

8. ***Life*** as used by Jesus is defined in John 17. Life is a relationship with God. It gives us that ability to know God relationally.

9. Read and summarize this section in the book.

10. This is a great question for discussion. Genesis teaches us that when Adam and Eve fell, they experienced death. Their bodies and souls began dying, and they immediately lost their relationship with God. Every person after them experienced physical and spiritual death until Jesus came to pay the penalty for sin so that he could reestablish a relationship with God for those who believe in him.

11. ***Death*** describes the loss of a relationship with God. See the book for more information.

WHY DID JESUS COME?

12. ***Zōē*** life is a relationship with God. Receiving this life allows God's original design for us to be restored. In a sense, because of the fall, we were living as two-dimensional creatures rather than three-dimensional creatures. We were designed to be most fulfilled when we live life with God. It is not until we have ***zōē*** life that we can live as God designed.

13. Discuss this question.

14. The way to receive ***zōē*** life is to believe. Believe means "reliant tust." We need to choose to reliantly trust in Jesus as our Savior from sin and as our God. As a result, he gives us the gift of forgiveness and life.

15. Discuss where your participants are in relation to embracing Jesus as Savior and God.

The Primary Purpose of the Church

Purpose - The goal of this lesson is to identify three primary truths about the church and see how they apply to us. In addition, we are trying to help people see and embrace the goal of the church, which is to work together to help make whole-life disciples of Jesus.

Insights for Each Question

1. This question is designed to get your participants talking about their opinions of what they think the church is before you begin the study.

2. Some common thoughts about the church are that it is programs, buildings, a place where hypocrites go, and so on.

3. The three biblical descriptions of the church are detailed below:

    a. Ephesians 1 – The church = Jesus as the head and believers as the body. The most important part is that Jesus is the leader of the church. This goes with the diagram on page 15.

    b. Ephesians 2 – The church is built on Jesus as the cornerstone (the first stone laid, which determines the rest of the building). The church is also built on the teaching of the apostles (the Bible). This goes with the diagram on page 15. Together, this is another picture of the church.

c. Ephesians 3 – The church is a combination of Jew and gentile. Both groups are fused into one in God's eyes when they believe in Jesus.

4. In summary, the church should live under the leadership of Jesus, be rightly related to him through following the teaching of the Bible, and be unified.

5. This is a question to interact over. One answer could be that Jesus left us here so that we could help each other become more like him.

6. The Great Commission reveals a PRIMARY (not the only) purpose of the church. Jesus left us here to go and make disciples in the world.

7. The command in this passage is "make disciples."

8. Jesus desires for us to go into the entire world and make disciples. He promises to be with us to help us in this process.

9. It is important to help people see that this command is for all believers, not just the apostles. (See the next question).

10. Acts 11:26 is an important verse that helps clarify question 9. This verse describes where the disciples were first called "Christians." This is important because the word *disciple* is not used after the book of Acts. The word *disciple*

transitioned to other words in the New Testament. Some of those words are *Christian, believer, brother, and sister.* So, since the word *disciple* is the same as *Christian*, we all need to be helping people become Christians. Therefore, we should all be making disciples.

11. The Holy Spirit is our helper to make disciples. Followers of Jesus should take his message to the world.

12. The important point to note here is the concept of comprehensive discipleship. This phrase refers to the truth that Jesus made whole-life disciples. In other words, being a disciple of Jesus should impact all of a person's life. Unfortunately, many discipleship approaches are programs or focus only on spiritual disciplines. Comprehensive discipleship means that every area of my life—work, marriage, parenting, spiritual growth, stewardship, and God's design to live out biblical manhood and womanhood—should be under his leadership.

13. Notice Wilkins' quote after this question.

14. Discuss what values a church could have to help accomplish comprehensive discipleship.

15. This question is a little hard for readers to figure out on their own.

    a. Hebrews 12 – "worship"

    b. 1 Peter 2 – "family"

    c. 2 Peter 3– "growth"

    d. Ephesians 4 – "service"

THE PRIMARY PURPOSE OF THE CHURCH

16. I need to become like Jesus in all of life. This will happen as I worship him, live as family with other believers, grow, and serve.

WHAT DOES IT MEAN TO BE A DISCIPLE OF JESUS?

Purpose - The goal of this lesson is to clarify the meanings of the words ***disciple***, ***discipleship***, and ***discipling***. We also want to help people understand how Jesus used the concept of the master/disciple relationship in existence in that culture.

INSIGHTS FOR EACH QUESTION

1. Read Appendix One.

2. Hit the highlights of Appendix One. Discuss what stood out to you and allow each person to share.

3. Wilkins defines the word *disciple* as "**coming** to Jesus alone for eternal life, **embracing** him as Savior and God, and **embarking** on the life of following him."1

4. Becoming a Christian includes the first two aspects of the above definition. Living as a disciple is the third aspect of the above definition.

   Embarking on the life of following Jesus includes 3 things:

   Committed follower

   Sustained relationship

   Imitation of conduct

   I remind people that an easy way to remember this acrostic is the TV show *CSI*.

WHAT DOES IT MEAN TO BE A DISCIPLE OF JESUS?

5. This is a question to interact over. The definitions we will use for these words are also included under this question in the book.

6. Although not mentioned in the text, this section shows how Jesus implemented CSI in his form of discipleship.

   a. Luke 9:23 explains what Jesus meant by the "C." It is dying to self and following Jesus.

   b. John 15:9-11 gives the rules for "S." To enjoy a sustained, loving relationship with Jesus, we need to follow his leadership as described in the Word.

   c. Galatians 4:19 explains the "I." Imitation of conduct means we look like Jesus over time.

7. This question is to get people sharing their thoughts before we explore the answer.

8. These two quotes help to clarify what it means for us to pick up our cross to follow Jesus. Those who were to be crucified in that day knew that once they picked up the cross, there was no hope for them. They were about to die. For the disciple of Jesus, the issue is allegiance. We choose to stop living for ourselves and our interests and seek to please Jesus first in our lives.

9. This is a great discussion question. Discuss where each person struggles with following Jesus.

10. All disciples have the goal of becoming like our teacher—Jesus.

WHAT DOES IT MEAN TO BE A DISCIPLE OF JESUS?

11. This last question is an opportunity to interact and then summarize the main points of the lesson. The following includes the main points to review:

    a. Make sure they know the definitions of disciple, discipleship, and discipling.

    b. Also, review what embarking on the life of following Jesus means. This is a reference to living out CSI on a moment-by-moment basis.

    c. Finally, help them leave with the understanding that following Jesus means living with a new approach to life: choosing to die to themselves and live for him above all else.

    d. You may also ask, "How are you doing with these concepts in your own life?"

Jesus' Approach to Discipleship

Purpose - The goal of this lesson is to help new disciples understand how Jesus did discipleship. Jesus did not create the master/disciple relationship. It was common for masters to have disciples at that time. Jesus used that concept and then adapted it to fit his purposes.

Insights for Each Question

1. It is important to see that Andrew and an unnamed disciple of John the Baptist chose to follow Jesus on their own initiative once John the Baptist identified Jesus as the Messiah. In that culture, anyone could choose to follow a master.

2. Read Matthew 4:18–20. Here you will see that Jesus calls two disciples to follow him. In verse 18, we see that those disciples are Andrew and Peter. We must remember that John 1:35–42 happened first. The reason they so quickly dropped everything to follow Jesus was that they had already been following him. This call entered a new phase of Jesus' form of discipleship. The formal call was not something other masters did at that time. This was new. The call demanded that a person choose to embrace Jesus as Savior and God or reject him.

3. Here we see that the proper response to the call was to follow, which is obedience. Nothing should challenge a disciple's allegiance to Jesus. In Matthew 4:18–20, we see the appropriate response to the call, and in

Matthew 19:21–22, we see the rejection of the call. Following accompanied belief.

4. In stage 3, Jesus sifts his followers. He begins to separate true believers from those who were just curious followers. He separates his followers by his teaching. True disciples follow.

5. Sometimes we might assume that the longer Jesus did discipleship, the number of his disciples significantly increased. We see in John 6 that many left him because they were not true believers. His process of challenging with the truth encouraged some to obey and follow, but it also caused many to leave. His form of discipleship actually decreased the number of his followers because he was concerned about quality, not quantity.

6. This question is designed to get people sharing their thoughts before exploring further.

7. Here we see there will be varying responses to the gospel. We should remember that everyone did not follow Jesus. In fact, most did not. Keep that in mind when you invest in the lives of others. Some will pan out, but many will not.

8. It is important to ask the new disciple, "What soil do you want to represent your life?" The difference in the soil is the response of our heart. Believe, be teachable, and be fruitful. That is the goal for all of us.

9. Discuss Appendix Two and hit the highlights. Ask the participants, "What stood out to you in the Appendix?" Being a disciple is much more than being a learner. It is a

life of following Jesus. Belief in Jesus is the starting line of discipleship, not the finish line.

10. When we share the gospel, we should not be afraid to discuss the cost. The possibility of being forgiven and receiving life cannot be earned. It is a free gift, but the life of following is expected and will cost everything we have. The gospel is free, but to embrace it costs a person's life.

11. This is simply a discussion question.

THE MARKS OF A DISCIPLE OF JESUS

Purpose - For a growing disciple, it is important to understand the key marks of a disciple of Jesus. Some give an endless list of things that should be true of a disciple, but Jesus said that three things would prove a person to be one of his disciples. We will try to understand what those things are so that we can seek to see them as realities in our lives.

INSIGHTS FOR EACH QUESTION

1. This is a question for interaction and discussion.

2. The first mark of a disciple is abiding or continuing in the words of Jesus. We stay within the teaching of Jesus and seek to follow his leadership through obedience to his Word.

3. The diagram in the column next to this question requires explanation. If we are to **abide** in the Word, that means the Word will teach us the truth. As we walk in the truth, it will also **reprove** us when we get off the path: the Word shows us when we error. The Word also **corrects** us, showing us how to get back on the path of the Word. Finally, the Word **trains** us for life.

4. It is hoped that the disciple can see that abiding in the Word is the primary way Jesus still leads us today.

5. It would be easy to get lost on this question. My hope is to stress the importance for the disciple to live in harmony with the teaching of Jesus. Such action shows we are his

disciples. If a person is not giving evidence of obeying the Word of Jesus, he is either a disobedient disciple or not a disciple at all.

6. As a follow-up to question five, we are not to judge others but to discern whether a person is living a life of obedience. If a person claims to be a disciple but is not living like it, we may have the opportunity to help him or her get back on the path of obedience or clarify how to become a disciple of Jesus.

7. Stress the need for the disciple to choose to follow Jesus by staying in his Word. We cannot control how others live, but we can control how we live.

8. This is a great discussion question to interact over.

9. The second mark of a disciple is love.

10. The answer to this question is in the gray column on the following page. Love is new because Jesus is the **new example**, we are in a **new family**, and we have a **new capacity** to love through the enabling of the Holy Spirit.

11. When we believe in Jesus, we become part of God's family. Our choice to follow and obey him should be expected of a family member. Love is the currency of family relationships. The comments under this question give further insight.

12. Love is action. Biblical love is activated by loving brothers and sisters in need and helping them carry burdens too heavy for them to carry on their own. Love is to be expressed toward believers and unbelievers.

13. Love is important because our Father loves by nature. We should act like our Father.

14. Fruit is the third mark of a disciple of Jesus.

15. The question that normally surfaces at this time is "What is fruit?" Fruit is action in harmony with the character of Jesus, and it also refers to a disciple's transformed character .

16. The fruit of a disciple should be the fruit of the Spirit.

    The explanations for questions 17 and 18 are found under each question.

17. This is a summary question for discussion.

How Do We Become Like Jesus?

Purpose - For a growing disciple, it is important to understand how to become like Jesus. Imitation of conduct is one of the expectations of his disciples. We are to become like him in all of life. The problem is that we cannot do this in our own power. This lesson will show how we are to be rightly related to the Spirit so that he can change us from the inside out to be more like Jesus.

Insights for Each Question

1. The Holy Spirit is the third person of the Trinity. You may want to go back to lesson one to look at the diagram of how God is one essence but exists in three unique persons. The Holy Spirit is the one who will give us power to witness and to change.

2. The Holy Spirit is the one who works within us to change us to look like Jesus.

3. We need the Spirit because we can't change ourselves. Even Paul discovered he could not change himself no matter how hard he tried. Thankfully, the Spirit is God's answer for us to experience life change.

4. It will take a lifetime to become like Jesus as we cooperate with the Holy Spirit to change us. We need the Spirit because we all still possess a fallen nature known as the flesh. The flesh is that desire within us to please ourselves more than God. We cannot overcome that desire on our

own. It takes the enabling of the Spirit to live righteously and to change.

5. Paul shows the problem in Romans 7 and answers it in Romans 8. See the comments under the question for further insight.

6. The answers to these questions are shown under #7 in the book.

7. See the comments under this question.

   Questions 8, 9, and 10 are explained in the book.

We should begin the practice of confessing sin as it is committed and then yield by faith to the enabling of the Spirit. Then walk by faith in the power and path (the Word) of the Spirit.

NEW RELATIONSHIPS: LIVING AS FAMILY

Purpose: It is important for disciples of Jesus to realize that we are not meant to live life alone. In fact, when we believe in Jesus as our Savior and God, we enter into the family of God. We become his children. That means all believers are our brothers and sisters. It is in the context of family relationships where God designed us to grow. The best place to find these relationships is in a local church. This lesson will help us understand God's plan for our growth in relationship with others.

INSIGHTS FOR EACH QUESTION

1. John 1:12 reveals that because of our new birth (John 3), we become part of a new family—the family of God. It is important to understand that although we all are creations of God, only those who believe in Jesus as Savior and God become God's children and part of his family.

2. Since all of us become children of God through Jesus, that makes us brothers and sisters. The terminology related to the word disciple transitioned to family terms, brother and sister, to emphasize the close relationship we share as disciples of Jesus.

3. If you and I will embrace the truth that we are brothers and sisters in God's family, then we should live accordingly. I need to make developing those relationships an important priority in my life.

4. Although we as individuals must abide in the Word, remain yielded to the Spirit, love, and produce fruit, we also must be relationally connected to other Christians. God designed us to flourish in relationship with other Christians. It is in relationship with others that I can grow up in love.

5. It is in relationship with others that I learn truth practically and in the real world. Truth is no longer a theory or an idea. It is with others that I learn how to live out my faith.

6. In 1 John 3:14 we learn that God is the source of all love. Since God is the source of love, we experience God's love for us practically through others.

7. Since love seeks only the good of others at our personal expense, the world will be intrigued when it sees Christians living in this way. In fact, in the early church it was a magnet that drew non-believers to consider the claims of Christ. If we do the same today, we can expect similar results.

8. Some characteristics of the Christian family are described in the following verses:

    a. Romans 15:7—Read this verse in the NLT version. We must unconditionally accept other Christians as Jesus accepted us.

    b. Colossians 3:16—We need to be teaching one another the Word.

    c. Galatians 6:2—We need to be helping other Christians when circumstances are too heavy for them to bear on their own.

d. Romans 14:19—We should be building one another up intentionally.

e. 1 Corinthians 12:25—We are to care for one another.

f. James 5:16—We need to confess our sins to and pray for one another.

g. Romans 12:10—We are to love and honor one another.

h. 1 Thessalonians 4:18—We are to encourage one another.

9. Although there can be many places you can find Christian relationships, God designed the church to be the primary place where those exist. It is important to find a Bible-believing, Bible-teaching church where you can get relationally connected and experience family the way God designed it.

10. The only way Christian family relationships will work is if we seek the interests of others above our own. Jesus modeled that for us in Philippians 2. We also need to understand that these relationships are God's design and not optional. They must become a priority in our lives.

11. It is important that we all figure out how we can be relationally connected to others so that we can become who Jesus wants us to be.

Developing Your Relationship with God

Purpose – Disciples of Jesus have the privilege of developing a relationship with him. One key aspect for growing in a relationship with Jesus is prayer. Prayer is simply talking to God, but learning how God expects us to pray is important. This lesson introduces some of the presumptions and limits of prayer. These concepts are important because there is such confusion on this topic today.

Insights for Each Question

1. This is a question for interaction. It appears that these men saw a great benefit to prayer.

2. Prayer is simply talking to God.

   Questions 3 and 4 are great discussion questions with some suggested answers in the book.

5. This is a very important question. Many people have not considered that there could actually be limits to prayer. Prayer has limits to what it can accomplish only if the Bible puts limits on it.

6. This passage is very easy to misunderstand. Read everything in the book on this question. Jesus is not saying that we can do whatever we want in prayer but that the first limit of prayer is faith. Since faith is a limit to prayer, it is important to understand what faith is. Faith is not believing that

whatever you want will happen. In Scripture, it is believing God will do what He promises.

Faith has an object (God) and a content (His promise or command). When we pray, we are simply trusting in God to do as he promised or asking him to help us live out his command.

7. The second limit to prayer is that it must be in harmony with God's will. God's will has been revealed in the Bible.

8. The third limit of prayer is that we must pray in the name of Jesus. Read what is in the book to explain this concept. Praying in the name of Jesus is not a magic formula that makes God give us what we ask; instead, it is a way for us to say that the requests we are asking are in harmony with Jesus and his character.

Questions 9 and 10 are great discussion questions.

Praying with Confidence

Purpose – After understanding the limits of prayer so that we can pray according to God's will, we must see how this applies to our lives in a practical way. This lesson is a general overview of types of prayer requests. This lesson does not discuss conversations with God but specific requests for things.

Insights for each question

1. The first type of prayer request is praying selfishly with impure motives. If we pray in this way, then we should not expect an answer to our prayer.

2. The second type of prayer has already been discussed in the previous lesson. It is prayer that is in harmony with God's will. We must simply meet any conditions of God's will before that prayer is answered.

3. The only way we can be certain of God's will is if he has communicated it in the Bible.

4. This is a great model prayer. He approaches God with praise exalting him for who he is. Then he reminds God of his past acts on the behalf of his people. Finally, he explains the problem and asks for God's help.

5. This is meant to be a discussion question. An example of a timeless promise would be Acts 16:31. The promise is that all who believe in Jesus as Savior and God will be saved from the penalty for their sin.

6. Here we see that Paul often longed to go to Rome and that he wanted to have his thorn in the flesh removed. Those prayers seemed good to him for his efforts in expanding the kingdom, but they were not answered the way he desired. This type of prayer, then, seems good to us and is in harmony with God's will as far as we know, but we do not know for sure if it is what God wants.

7. Here we need to see that most of our prayer fits in this last category, and we need to learn how to pray for it.

8. In this third category, we pray what is on our hearts, but we yield these requests to God's will, trusting that he knows best. The fruit of this prayer is that we will be in harmony with God's will.

9. This is a great question for discussion. See the book for suggestions on how to walk through this section.

10. We must let go of something in order to really throw it. In prayer, we must give our concern to God and trust him rather than hold onto it and try to twist his arm to do our will. Yield to his will and trust him. Let go of it so that we can experience his peace.

11. This is a discussion question with the answer in the book.

12. This is a discussion question.

The chart at the end of this lesson is a summary showing that when we pray according to this third type of prayer, God is the object of our prayer. The content of our prayer is his promise, his command, or his character. When there is no promise, then we place our trust in his character.

LIVING BY FAITH RATHER THAN FEELINGS

Purpose – God has created us as emotional beings. Feelings are important, but we need to explore how our feelings relate to living the Christian life. All of us have had times when we did not feel like a Christian or did not feel close to God. How do those feelings relate to following Jesus?

INSIGHTS FOR EACH QUESTION

1. Disciples need to understand that if feelings determine their obedience and faithfulness to Jesus, then they will have a very up and down Christian experience.

2. Hebrews 11 is a famous chapter in the Bible on faith. Often it is described as the hall of faith. Faith is choosing to do God's will regardless of how we feel.

3. The definition of faith is in the book.

4. If faith is "reliant trust in God to achieve his promises," then we need to live moment by moment in that way. The disciple should learn the slogan "faith it till you feel it." The point here is that we place our faith in God and his promises and choose to live faithfully, regardless of how we feel.

5. This is a discussion question with the answer in the book.

6. This is a discussion question.

7. There are three things to see here. First, in 2 Peter, we can see that God worked through the writers of Scripture, allowing them to use their unique personalities, but the result was the very thing God wanted written down. Second, 2 Timothy shows that the Bible describes the result of this process as inspiration. God inspired his Word. The third truth to observe, in the book of Numbers, is that God does not lie. Therefore, we can have complete confidence in God and his Word if we embrace those three things.

8. Simply discuss the Appendix with insights you saw or interact over what the participants learned.

9. This question lists a number of verses that encourage us to trust God regardless of how we feel:

    - Psalm 90:2 – God has always been. He is eternal.
    - Isaiah 40:13–14 – God know everything. He does not have to learn anything.
    - Joshua 24:19; Psalm 99:3; Isaiah 40:25 – God is a holy God, and no one compares to him.
    - Malachi 3:6; James 1:17 – God is faithful: he gives us every good thing we have.
    - 1 Kings 8:27 – Creation cannot contain God.
    - 1 John 4:8 – God is love.
    - Genesis 17:1 – God is sovereign and is in control of all things.
    - Psalm 139:7–11
    - Psalm 139:16 – God created me just as I am and knows me intimately.

- Psalm 11:7 – God is just.
- John 4:24 – God is Spirit.
- John 17:3 – God cannot lie, and eternal life is a relationship with him that goes on forever.

10. This is a great discussion question.
11. This diagram is to be explained as follows: The **engine** is what pulls the train. The facts refer to the Bible, which is our engine. Faith, the **coal car**, feeds the engine. Our faith must be in the facts. The caboose does not pull the train. The **caboose** is part of the train but follows faith placed in the facts. Feelings do not determine our obedience or lack of obedience.
12. This is meant to be a discussion question.

READING THE WORD TO CHANGE

Purpose – The second way to develop our relationship with God is through reading his Word. His Word is our guide for life. The problem with many disciples is that they know more than they live. The life of a disciple is to be one lived like Jesus, not a life that simply knows how Jesus lived life. The issue is, how do we read the Bible to change and not just to accumulate facts?

This lesson is not an exhaustive description of how to read or study the Bible. This lesson only focuses on how we can read the Bible to change—to see the facts move from our head to our heart.

INSIGHTS FOR EACH QUESTION

1. This is a discussion question.

2. The Bible's role in our life is described in the following Bible chapters:

    - Colossians 3 – The Word is to dwell in us.
    - 2 Timothy 3 – The Word is profitable for teaching, training, reproof, and correction.
    - 2 Timothy 2 – We must work hard at studying the Word.

3. Interact over this problem. The goal for the disciple of Jesus is to change to become more like him. This means we have to change. We have to learn how he wants us to live, and then we must turn that knowledge into heart change.

4. Interact over this problem. The biggest obstacle to life change is our selfish desires. We must continually die to ourselves to live for God. Also notice that the chart introduces a five-step process for applying the Bible to life.

5. This is a discussion question. In my experience, many people skip step four in the previous chart. We move from discovering facts to application rather than taking time to reflect over the truths learned so that these timeless truths can move from our heads to our hearts.

6. This is a discussion question.

7. This is a discussion question. The chart here is an expansion of step four in the previous chart. It helps us reflect and marinate on God's Word and how it applies to us.

   Questions 8, 9, and 10 are discussion questions.

As you conclude the lesson, review the whole book and interact over what most impacted them personally. Take the opportunity to discuss next steps as you follow Jesus together.

ENDNOTES

1. WHY DID JESUS COME?

1. R. C. H. Lenski, *The Interpretation of St. John's Gospel* (Minneapolis: Augsburg Publishing House, 1961), 30.
2. William Hendriksen and Simon J. Kistemaker, John 1:1 in *New Testament Commentary: Exposition of the Gospel According to John, New Testament Commentary* Vol. 1–2 (Grand Rapids: Baker Book House, 1953–2001), 70.
3. Tom Constable, John 1:1 in *Tom Constable's Expository Notes on the Bible* CD-ROM (Garland, TX: Galaxie Software, 2003).
4. Spiros Zodhiates, *The Complete Word Study Dictionary: New Testament* (Chattanooga: AMG Publishers, 2000).
5. Zodhiates, *The Complete Word Study Dictionary: New Testament*.
6. For further discussion of this word, see Gerhard Kittel, Gerhard Friedrich, and Geoffrey William Bromiley, *Theological Dictionary of the New Testament* (Grand Rapids: W. B. Eerdmans, 1985), 294.
7. John H. Walton, Mark L. Strauss, and Ted Cooper, *The Essential Bible Companion: Key Insights for Reading God's Word* (Grand Rapids: Zondervan, 2006), 9.
8. Biblical Studies Press, Note on John 17:3 in *The NET Bible First Edition* (Richardson, TX: Biblical Studies Press, 2005), 2084.

2. THE PRIMARY PURPOSE OF THE CHURCH

1. Michael J. Wilkins, *The NIV Application Commentary: Matthew*, ed. Terry Muck (Grand Rapids: Zondervan, 2004), 951.
2. Michael J. Wilkins, *Following the Master: A Biblical Theology of Discipleship* (Grand Rapids: Zondervan, 1992), 299.
3. Wilkins, *Following the Master*, 124.

3. WHAT DOES IT MEAN TO BE A DISCIPLE OF JESUS?

1. Wilkins, *Following the Master*, 40.

2. D. A. Carson, Feb. 5 Reading in ***For the Love of God: A Daily Companion for Discovering the Riches of God's Word.*** Vol. 1 (Wheaton, IL: Crossway Books, 1998).
3. J. P. Moreland and Klaus Issler, ***The Lost Virtue of Happiness: Discovering the Disciplines of the Good Life*** (Colorado Springs: NavPress, 2006), 30.

4. JESUS' APPROACH TO DISCIPLESHIP

1. Wilkins, ***Following the Master***, 84–107. For great insight into this process, see chapter six.
2. Wilkins, ***Following the Master***, 110.
3. Wilkins, ***Following the Master***, 84–107.

5. THE MARKS OF A DISCIPLE OF JESUS

1. George R. Beasley-Murray, ***Word Biblical Commentary: John***, WordBiblical Commentary vol. 36 (Dallas: Word, Inc., 2002), 133.

6. HOW DO WE BECOME LIKE JESUS?

1. J. Dwight Pentecost, ***The Divine Comforter: The Person and Work of the Holy Spirit*** (Grand Rapids: Kregel Publications, 1997), 154.
2. Pentecost, ***The Divine Comforter***, 157.
3. For further discussion on this topic, please see Pentecost, ***The Divine Comforter***, 158.
4. Eldon Woodcock, "The Filling of the Holy Spirit." ***Bibliotheca Sacra*** 157, no. 625 (January 2000): 68–87.

7. NEW RELATIONSHIPS: LIVING AS FAMILY

1 Joe Hellerman, "When the Church Was a Family: Revisioning Christian Community in Light of Ancient Social Values." For Talbot School of Theology, 50th Anniversary Faculty Monograph, 4.

2 Hellerman, 4–5.

3 Klaus Issler, Wasting Time with God: A Christian Spirituality of Friendship with God (Downers Grove, Ill.: Intervarsity Press, 2001), 57.

4 Wilkins, 233.

5 Joseph Hellerman, When the Church Was a Family: Recapturing Jesus' Vision for Authentic Christian Community (Nashville: B&H Publishing, 2009), 1.

6 Hellerman, Monograph, 7.

8. DEVELOPING YOUR RELATIONSHIP WITH GOD

1. Oswald Chambers, Oct. 17 reading in ***My Utmost for His Highest: Selections for the Year*** (Grand Rapids: Oswald Chambers Publications, 1986).
2. Wayne R. Spear, ***Talking to God: The Theology of Prayer*** (Pittsburgh: Crown & Covenant, 2002), 7.
3. Spear, ***Talking to God***, 57.
4. Spear, ***Talking to God***, 57.
5. Donald Burdick, ***The Epistles of John*** (Chicago: Moody Press, 1970), 92.
6. John Stott, ***The Letters of John*** (Westmont, IL: IVP Academic, 2009), 188.
7. Spear, ***Talking to God***, 59.
8. Note on John 14:13–14, ESV® Bible (The Holy Bible, English Standard Version®). ESV® Permanent Text Edition® (2016). Copyright © 2001 by Crossway, a publishing ministry of Good News Publishers. Used by permission. All rights reserved.
9. Warren W. Wiersbe, ***The Bible Exposition Commentary***, Vol. 1 (Wheaton, IL: Victor Books, 1996), 419.
10. E. M. Bounds, ***Winning the Invisible War*** (Pittsburgh: Whittaker House, 1984), 150.

9. PRAYING WITH CONFIDENCE

1. E. M. Bounds, ***The Works of E. M. Bounds*** (Zeeland, MI: Reformed Church Publications, 2009), 29.
2. Andrew Murray, ***The Prayer Life*** ebook (Amazon Digital Services, LLC, 2010), 4.
3. John Calvin, ***Institutes of the Christian Religion, Book III*** (Carlisle, PA: Banner of Truth, 2014 [1541]), 27.

10. LIVING BY FAITH RATHER THAN FEELINGS

1. Bill Bright, ***A Handbook For Christian Maturity***, (Peachtree City: Campus Crusade For Christ, 1994), 442.

11. READING THE WORD TO CHANGE

1. William Hendriksen and Simon J. Kistemaker, ***Exposition of Philippians***, vol. 5, New Testament Commentary (Grand Rapids: Baker Book House, 2001), 200.

APPENDIX ONE: THE MEANING OF MATHETES (DISCIPLE)

1. Kay Arthur and Tom and Jane Hart, ***Being a Disciple: Counting the Real Cost*** (Colorado Springs: Waterbrook Press, 2001), 11.
2. Wilkins, ***Following the Master***, 78.
3. Wilkins, ***Following the Master***, 40.
4. Michael J. Wilkins, ***In His Image: Reflecting Christ in Everyday Life*** (Colorado Springs: NavPress, 1997), 112.
5. George Barna, ***Growing True Disciples*** (Colorado Springs: WaterBrook, 2001), 54.

APPENDIX TWO: AN INCOMPLETE GOSPEL

1. Dietrich Bonhoeffer, ***The Cost of Discipleship*** (New York: Touchstone; 1995), 11.
2. Keith Matthews, "The Transformational Process," in ***The Kingdom Life: A Practical Theology of Discipleship and Spiritual Formation***, ed. Alan Andrews (Colorado Springs: NavPress, 2010),86.
3. Wilkins, ***Following the Master: A Biblical Theology of Discipleship***, 104–113. Wilkins supports this view and proves that following Jesus as his disciple was different from all other forms of master/disciple relationships in that day because of his call to believe, which includes the expectaiton to follow.
4. Wilkins, ***Following the Master***, 109.

5. John Stott, foreword to ***Side by Side: A Handbook: Disciple Making for a New Generation***, by Steve and Lois Rabey (Colorado Springs: NavPress, 2000), 7.
6. J. P. Moreland and Klaus Issler, ***The Lost Virtue of Happiness: Discovering the Disciplines of the Good Life*** (Colorado Springs: NavPress, 2006), 30.
7. Steve and Lois Rabey, ***Side by Side: A Handbook: Disciple Making for a New Generation*** (Colorado Springs: NavPress, 2000), 213.
8. Mitzi Miller, ***Chocolate Chip Cookie versus a Brownie*** (Paper, Fellowship Bible Church, Little Rock, AR, April 6, 2006).
9. Wilkins, ***Following the Master***, 238.

APPENDIX THREE: THE CHALLENGE OF THE FLESH

1. William Barclay, ***The New Daily Bible Study: The Letter to the Romans*** (Philadelphia: Westminster Press, 2002), 98.

APPENDIX FOUR: THE MOST UNIQUE BOOK EVER WRITTEN

1. James Emery White, ***Can We Trust the Bible?*** (Downers Grove, IL: InterVarsity Press, 2010), 1.
2. Ken Boa and Larry Moody, ***I'm Glad You Asked*** (Colorado Springs: Victor, 1994), 100.
3. Josh McDowell, ***Evidence That Demands a Verdict*** (Nashville: Thomas Nelson,1999),193.
4. Norman L. Geisler and Ronald M. Brooks, ***When Skeptics Ask*** (Wheaton, IL: Victor Books, 1990), 154.

LEADERS' GUIDE

1. Michael J. Wilkins, ***Following Jesus: A Biblical Theology of Discipleship*** (Grand Rapids: Zondervan, 1992), 40.

Made in United States
North Haven, CT
25 August 2022

23246336R00076